On Wings
of Prayer

On Wings
of Prayer

Revd Dr David Thompson

ISBN 978-0-9562190-2-2

About the Author

David Thompson was first aware of the presence of the living God as a child in the war years. On leaving school he spent three dreary years in accountancy and banking and was saved from becoming a stuffed shirt in the city by the call to ordination.

For the next seven years he engaged in full time study reading theology at King's College London and Christ Church Oxford. He says that he acquired a healthy tan through the windows of the Vatican library while pursuing his liturgical studies in Rome.

While in London he was inspired by the teaching and preaching of the Chaplain the Revd G. L. Phillips. He was married in 1965 and was prepared for the priesthood at St Stephen's House. Two curacies and a short incumbency at the village of Braughing followed, after which he became Team Rector of Digswell.

In 1970 he supported John Pringle in his efforts to establish the National Schizophrenia Fellowship (now called Rethink) and served on the Council/Trustees until 1997.

A Pentecostal experience in 1960 lit a long fuse which eventually led to the development of services of Worship and Healing and the initiation of services of Pentecost Praise in St Alban's Abbey.

An extraordinary gift day in church in 1994 enabled a group to purchase a house near the church for community and healing. This faith venture continued for seven years. From this group emerged the Rose of Sharon Society, currently a group of some forty lay people committed to prayer.

He retired in 1998 to pray and lives in the Janitor's cottage in a little village in the north east of Scotland.

Contents

Preface

And all the people said Amen.[1]

The Amen was the seal on the great prayer of King David as he praised God for the arrival of the ark in Jerusalem and gave thanks to God, "because he is good and his mercy endures forever."[2]

Some years ago my brother Patrick suggested that I write something for the Church of England. I decided I couldn't do this. Rapidly shifting sands indicated that even if I had something to say, which was far from certain, it would in any case soon be out of date. But even as I put the suggestion aside, I found myself reflecting upon the importance of the role of live and active prayer.

Jesus prayed without ceasing. As a praying presence in the temple he was deeply moved by what he saw and cried aloud, "My house shall be called a house of prayer."[3]

Today we pass the turnstiles of a great cathedral and find ourselves in a shop full of bric-a-brac. We attend a prayer group, where we are assured that God will bless us, but fail to learn that there are challenging things to be done. And even in our secret place of prayer, the words we mumble can't always be equated with a heart centred on God.

To help us to grow spiritually we turn to the Gospels. There we find a remarkable consistency between what Jesus said and what he did. He taught us to pray. He devoted his life to prayer. He was up betimes to pray. He climbed the mountain to pray. He was at prayer at the Last Supper, in the Garden of Gethsemane and on the Cross. Jesus prayed without ceasing.

If we want to grow in prayer we make prime time,[4] so that we begin to live a life charged with the glory of God and aflame with his love.

The spiritual life involves the whole man: body, mind and spirit. We can no more reduce spiritual life to a physical activity of the brain, than conclude that there is no more going on when I write these words other than the electronic activities in my computer. Going to work on Monday morning is spiritual as well as natural. Because it isn't easy to see where one ends and the other begins is no good reason for ignoring either. To ignore the spiritual is to be only half alive.

In the life of genuine prayer the eye of the soul is gradually opened. We see a panoramic view. We see new dimensions. We see God's love within and all around us.

"On Wings of Prayer" is as mixed as a sherry trifle and was made with a good deal of assistance from members of the Rose of Sharon Society, a small band of the faithful, who live in the world and are devoted to prayer.

I have used words such as heart, mind, soul and spirit, in a traditional and devotional sense. I have used the word "men" and "man" inclusively, taking my cue from the book of Genesis, which first tells us that, "God made man in his own image," before going on to say, "Male and female created he them."[5]

It is half a century since I went to see my great uncle, Canon Francis Mercer, a former missionary in Japan and Canada, and a devoted parish priest in Leeds. I heard him chuckling with joy as he walked down the corridor to answer the door. When I told him I was about to be ordained he was silent for a moment before saying,

> "There is so much that I now find it hard to accept but of one thing I am absolutely certain – the reality of the living Christ."

Alleluia, He is risen indeed. Our vocation is to commune with him, to hear his voice and to second his proposals.

David Thompson
Advent 2010

Notes

1. I Chronicles 16.36.
2. 1 Chronicles 16.34.
3. Matthew 21.13.
4. Prime time is not just the remains of the day, but time when we are alert and active. It is quality time – not bed time.
5. Genesis 1.26–27.

Chapter One

Your servant is listening

"None of us is perfect!"

This was the mantra of one of my sons when corrected. He was right. God alone is good and by that standard we all fall short, but this is no excuse for complacently colluding with the less good part of our human nature, mumbling something obscure about the darker side, and making no effort to improve!

Saintly people have always been aware of their imperfections. John Vianney[1] knew he was an indifferent Latin scholar and a hopeless soldier, but these failures were overlooked by the Church and he exercised a saintly ministry in the little village of Ars. This holy priest, who had such insight into souls and lived a highly disciplined life, was often heard to say that he longed to leave his parish to go away, "to weep over his own poor life."

Closer to home the eccentric Christian writer, G.K. Chesterton,[2] well known for his criticism of big business, technology, and the monolithic state, and author of a little book called *Orthodoxy*, replied to a question he read in a letter to a newspaper, "What is wrong with this country?" by responding, "I am."

The two great commandments

Prayer is listening to God. Prayer is accepting his help, while learning and re-learning the basic rule of Christian living summed up in a few words by our Lord Jesus Christ, "Love one another as I have loved you."[3]

Under the direction of the Holy Spirit we immerse ourselves in the Gospel, where we discover that there is more to Christian living than warm fuzzy feelings. Costly experience teaches us that if we attempt to live the Gospel life without the grace of God, our endeavours will fail as quickly as a New Year's resolution.

Prayer isn't an idle avoidance of all challenges. If we waste time wool gathering, worrying, wallowing in self pity or floating aimlessly in a purple haze, it won't be long before we sink into the quicksands of despair. If we make achieving our self-centred personal ambitions our one aim in life, regardless of the needs of others and heedless of the Gospel, spiritual growth will falter as we become narcissistic and boring.

To pray is to commune with the King of Love. The purpose of prayer is to be so enriched by his love that we are changed. To bring about that change we do all that we can to keep the two great commandments of Jesus Christ:

> To love the Lord your God with all your heart, with all your soul, with all your strength, and with all your mind.
>   and
> To love your neighbour as yourself.[4]

Christian prayer lubricates the hinges of the door of the soul. Christian prayer welcomes the King of Glory in. Christian prayer is receptive and willing to see our human love transformed by his most perfect love. Transformed love issuing in the most precious fruits of obedience is the best evidence that prayer is real. To pray, then, is to retain a continuing focus both on God and on what God requires of us.

Disciplined prayer helps us not to be distracted but, "to hear the word of God and to do it."[5]

The love of God is spontaneous and enduring. Far from inhibiting our personal freedom, it helps us to be who we really are and to flourish in the place where he has called us to be.

Ross

Ross, a wayward but lovable donkey, lived for a while in the vicarage garden. When he was bored, he hopped over the electric fence and set off for the village. I often had to search for him and bring him back.

On one occasion late on a winter's night, a desire for the good life took him to the main street. He was spotted rolling around in the snow on his back, on the threshold of the village pub. The startled look of dazed unbelief on the face of the villager who came to the vicarage door to report his antics, was a sight. I set out to find Ross but as soon as I approached, he darted off. He disappeared across the fields past the village hall and was soon out of sight. Eventually I caught up with him happily trotting along the lane to a neighbouring village. I grabbed his halter and led him through the starlit night along a quiet country lane back to the vicarage. It was two o'clock in the morning before I got to bed.

On another occasion a hunger for adventure caused Ross to be lost in a vast Hertfordshire cornfield. At first I couldn't see him anywhere. Then I saw two grey cloth ears in the far distance, peaking up above acres of waving corn. I crawled behind cover and pounced. As I led a not-so-penitent donkey back to the village, I was greeted by curious villagers, who just happened to be assembled in their front gardens.

In Holy Week it was decided that Ross would have the honour of leading the Palm Sunday procession. He was parked overnight in a field near the church, so that he would be rested and refreshed for his big day. The presence of a lady donkey in the field next door was too much. He couldn't resist the temptation and jumped the fence.

The next morning he had to be caught and attended to by the vet, before walking shamefully down the village street at the head of the Palm Sunday procession, his ears and legs swathed in bandages. Ross was seriously wayward but I found it hard to be angry. Nevertheless, he found it difficult to accept that he was not free to do whatever he liked. There were constraints on his freedom. The electric fence wasn't there to punish him with a nasty shock, but to remind him to stay put in the shelter of the vicarage garden.

Ross's boundary was an electric fence. The boundaries for Christians are set by the Gospel of Christ. Our boundary is the way of Christ.

Prayer is fuelled by the Gospel. Prayer helps us to focus so that we don't repeat the same mistakes. Prayer is seeking the grace to stay in the corner of the Christian vineyard where we are supposed to be. How often do we foolishly gaze over the electric fence, lured by the attractions of the world, rather than labouring contentedly in the quiet corner where we are called to serve?

Nevertheless, our failures and wanderings shouldn't give rise to scruples or endless complaints about how awful we are. When we fail it is better to be humble. Ross the donkey didn't run away. On Palm Sunday morning he was there. He marched sheepishly down the high street. The bandages on his legs and ears told the story of a wayward night but they didn't put him off. He humbly led the procession to Church on Palm Sunday morning.

Men pleasers

Prayer is also hampered if we aren't where we are supposed to be because we give way to the wrongful demands of others and hunger for approval, rather than seconding God's proposals.

When Augustine, the future Bishop of Hippo, accepted an invitation to the Roman games, he might have thought that he could somehow remain uncontaminated by the horrid displays in the amphitheatre. Because he was pressured by his young friends, his doubts were set aside. Later, he was appalled by the effects of the atrocities on his soul. He learned the lesson that "bad company corrupts good manners."[6]

Christian prayer is becoming attuned to God's communications. It helps us to move beyond pleasing ourselves or seeking the approval of others, as we learn to be like the sheepdog lying on the rug in his appointed place in the corner of the farmhouse kitchen. He is still and silent. He keeps one ear cocked so that he stirs long before his master comes through the door. He hears the car door close and recognises his master's footsteps on the paving stones; he springs to attention the moment the good shepherd comes in.

Buy an alarm clock

Students at London University were told by the chaplain that there were choices to be made when you become a Christian. One of the first things to do was to go to the shops, buy an alarm clock and get up in the morning.

If we are serious about Christian living, it is essential to be disciplined about the management of time – going to bed, getting up, going to work refreshed, not neglecting the housework and saying our prayers. Doing things decently and in good order helps us to focus on God.

The discipline of prayer lies at the heart of the Christian life. Not to pray is as wanton as never speaking to your wife or never talking to your child. It is from our brief conversations with God in set times of prayer that continuous prayer will develop naturally.

Charles de Foucauld[7] lived a dissipated life as a lieutenant of the cavalry before he was brought back to the Christian faith and became a priest. After a period as a Trappist, he travelled to Algeria where he became known as the hermit of the Sahara. In scorching heat and blistering sand he spent his days in prayer, penance and works of charity. Although he lived a life of ceaseless prayer, he knew that the foundations for continuing prayer are laid by a disciplined approach to set times of prayer. Continuing, unceasing, or perpetual prayer he describes as follows:

> "If we are working at anything in the presence of one we love, we cannot forget his presence for a moment. Our eyes are on him constantly and the time passes quickly and happily. The hours given up entirely to prayer will give us the strength, with God's grace, to keep ourselves in his presence the rest of the day and give up all our time to what is called perpetual prayer."[8]

Prayer requires a certain amount of effort. Like any worthwhile activity, there are times when it is a struggle, but there are ample rewards. St Teresa of Avila, a contemplative who combined the life of prayer with an energetic and costly ministry as she built up the discalced Carmelites, wrote,

> "A soul in a real state of recollection is in a real paradise, because it walks with God, and is becoming more and more united with him."[9]

What legacy?

I had hardly sat down when the telephone rang. Could it be family or friends, I wondered, or was it one of those irritating interruptions? Maybe it was a cold caller trying to persuade me to change my energy supplier and planning to entice me into making out yet another direct debit. It was none of these. A mellifluous voice said, "Do you know that there are thousands of people in this country who have never made a will?"

This wasn't news to me so, not a little annoyed, I put down the phone as gently as I could. However, the question continued to echo around my mind. What is our legacy? What do we leave behind when we die?

My thoughts drifted back to my wedding day, when I stood before the priest and uttered the words, "With all my worldly goods I thee endow." After the service, my father had taken me quietly aside and told me that he had found it difficult not to raise an objection. He had been sorely tempted to stand up and say, "What worldly goods?" He had a good point. At the time of my marriage I didn't have a bean. The piggy bank was empty. I was a penniless student who would continue to be a penniless student for a further two years before becoming an even more impoverished curate.

The legacy of Peter, James and John wasn't a scientific discovery, a hoard of gold, a great work of art, literature or music, and didn't include the architectural treasures of Jerusalem or Rome. They handed down the enduring legacy of the Gospel. The mellifluous voice didn't persuade me to make another will but to ask a few questions.

What will I pass on to my children and grandchildren? What will I leave behind when I go? Will it be just a few oddments in the attic or a little cash? Will it be one or two family heirlooms and a few dusty books, or will it be the enduring fruits of faith, hope and love? As we consider our legacy we wonder if we are anything like the person God hoped we might become, and whether we have begun to respond to the injunction to store up treasure in heaven.[10] We examine ourselves to see if we are in the right place and about his business.

As we ponder who we are becoming, we try to imagine the kind of person God formed us to be. We yearn to fulfil our potential. We are overwhelmed by the thought that every person who ever existed or ever will exist is unique, chosen and precious. There can only ever be one me. No one else can be me or do what God requires of me, for not even clones can occupy the same space at the same time!

Inspiration

To help us to become our true selves we turn to the precious pages of the Gospels. There we see an account of Jesus surrounded by a crowd and we wonder why. As we pause for a moment, we notice him laying his hands upon the sick and speaking with authority to the crowds. We see a leper return to give thanks and a lame man healed. We see a young girl rise from her bed and a demoniac set free. We look again and behold huge crowds gathering because they have never known such teaching before. We do not withdraw our gaze as we watch the drama of Holy Week unfold and we realise that this is a man who spoke and lived the truth, whose actions always confirmed his words. This is a good man, we conclude; his teaching is like that of no other and his spiritual authority supreme. Then we see him walk the way of the Cross and die a brutal, unjust death.

Is this the end?

Thomas wasn't with the other disciples when they saw the risen Lord. He refused to accept their testimony and retired into his shell. But St John's Gospel gives an account of the memorable moment when everything fell into place. Thomas saw, believed and uttered a cry of joy and anguish: "My Lord and my God."[11]

Different Greek words for "seeing" in St John's Gospel[12] suggest that the seeds of faith were sown when Thomas first saw a quick glimpse of Jesus, and his faith began to increase when he beheld him. As he watched attentively, the drama unfolded like a spectacle in the theatre. Thomas was aware of widespread acclaim and growing hostility. Still he didn't really believe. After the Resurrection, he was distraught until the day he saw the risen Christ with his own eyes and finally saw and believed. He was overwhelmed by love. The puzzle was solved. Jesus was raised from the dead. The denouement was like seeing a circle form as sides are added to a multisided polygon, or the joy experienced the moment we know we have fallen in love.

The eye of the soul

On a still day, the garden was transformed. It was a garden which I recall was adorned with clouds of butterflies in the glorious summer of 1947. As I stood there, still weak and frail after a childhood illness, it was not the beauty of nature I saw, but the beauty of nature steeped in heavenly glory. One moment I was in an ordinary garden, the next I was in a paradise. I wouldn't have used these words at the time, but this mystical glimpse of nature charged with the grandeur of God is still imprinted on my mind.

Faith is trusting God. Faith is trusting his communications. Faith is a willingness to see and believe. Faith steps out into the darkness to find and lose ourselves in the immeasurable love of Christ. Faith is supremely exemplified in the "yes" of Mary, in her immediate and generous response to her extraordinary encounter with the angel Gabriel. She didn't sit down and write a long list of all the pros and cons of saying yes or no. She didn't even go in search of a rabbi to confirm her decision. She listened to her conscience which said yes, yes, a thousand times yes, for in her heart of hearts she knew what God required of her. It was a courageous and intuitive decision. Mary didn't even check with Joseph before she uttered her decisive fiat, "Behold the handmaid of the Lord. Be it unto me according to thy word."[13]

Cardinal Newman noted that if we try to build our faith upon reason and ignore the intuitive, we will never attain the certainty required to make a leap of faith.[14] The mind will be as restricted as a hobbled horse. We will be like Faulkland[15] in Sheridan's play *The Rivals*, who was constantly tormented by doubt about whether his lady really loved him. He was endlessly looking for confirmations, when it was obvious that she was devoted to him!

Seconding God's proposals

Jesus taught us to be faithful in little things.[16] Jesus taught us to be content to go and sit in the lowest place and remain there until we are requested to move up higher.[17] Our vocation isn't to save the planet. That responsibility belongs to God. Our responsibility isn't even to save ourselves for that too is in his hands. Our vocation is much simpler. It is, in the words of Florence Nightingale, to second God's proposals. For that remarkable lady this involved many things from inventing the pie chart to revolutionising nursing; from being an avid student of the Bible, prayer, St John of the Cross, and St Teresa of Avila to lobbying parliament in her works of mercy, reconciliation and healing.

As we embark upon the life of prayer, we rejoice that it is the will of God that we enter into the fullness of his love. It is foolish to decline this invitation to enter the place of freedom and peace. It is foolish to pout in our tents and despise his commands.[18] Rather we should rejoice in God's solemn promise to be with us now and until the end of time.[19]

Praying presence

When I was in college, I considered the possibility that I might become a hospital chaplain and was advised to meet the elderly chaplain of the Radcliffe hospital. He was far from well and his ministry was almost at an end. Nevertheless, I thought he would give me a blow-by-blow account of a typical day. To my surprise, when I met him he summed up his ministry as follows: "I try to be a praying presence in the hospital."

I had hoped that he would present me with an outline timetable. I thought that he would tell me when he was in chapel and who he visited. I had expected to hear him talk about the way he ministered to doctors and nurses and how he related to the hospital, the local church and the wider community. He did all of these things, but the bedrock of his ministry was prayer.

Later on I discovered that he was well known as a man of prayer in the hospital. Doctors who were performing tricky and complex surgery would call him to the operating theatre. They wanted him to be there because they knew the healing peace of his presence.

The work is the prayer

Those who are naturally industrious sometimes find it difficult to accept that prayer really matters. They think of it as a hasty one-sided monologue, to be attended to as quickly as possible, before scurrying here, there and everywhere, trying to do everything under their own steam.

But the maxim, "The work is the prayer" is only true insofar as the work is inspired by and flows from authentic prayer.

The notion that the work is the prayer may mislead us by suggesting that activity is everything and prayer is at best secondary, unnecessary or even a waste of time. If our good works aren't the fruit of humble prayer and fervent praise, they soon become egotistical self-indulgences.

Nevertheless, authentic prayer always issues in good works. Thomas Merton[20] wrote that prayer isn't only to be seen in the chapel but it is manifested in the way the monk wields a broom.

We are not alone

When we pray we are never alone because we are caught up in the intercessions of the saints and are privileged to participate in the worship of the whole company of heaven. Our prayer is a miniscule part of a chorus of unceasing praise, thanksgiving and intercession.

Even our own humble prayers know no bounds. We pray for ourselves and for our own needs. We pray for our homes, families and all those whom we love. We pray for the communities in which we live. We pray for our nation. We pray for the world. We pray for all those for whom the Holy Spirit inspires us to pray. We pray for the sick, the lonely and the unloved. We pray in season and out of season. We pray for our enemies. We pray in the Spirit. The Holy Spirit prays in us.

Prayer is life changing. Prayer works. I have often heard it said that positive answers to prayer are coincidences, but I have noted that when prayer is missing, coincidences go away! And in any case the word coincidence doesn't explain anything, it merely draws our attention to the observation that two things occur concurrently.

Prayer is a voyage of love and self discovery. In this journey we are assured of the support and guidance of the Holy Spirit who enables us to become more truly the person God has called us to be, as we develop deeper insight into who we really are and what makes us tick.

Speak Lord

Rather than turning over, taking no notice and going to sleep when God calls, it is better to follow the example of the child Samuel. As he lay fast asleep in the temple he heard a voice calling. He was deeply troubled and didn't know who it was or what to do. Distressed, he got up and ran across to find Eli the wise old priest, who advised him to say,

"Speak Lord for your servant is listening."[21]

This is what Samuel did. We do well to follow his example.

Notes

1. John Vianney. 1786–1859. By 1859 it is estimated that the number of visitors to Ars was 20,000 a year and that he spent sixteen to eighteen hours a day in the confessional. See Lancelot Shepherd, *The Curé d'Ars*. Burns and Oates. 1958. pp. 13–28.
2. G.K. Chesterton. Became a Roman Catholic in 1922. Author of *Orthodoxy*, and the well loved Father Brown stories.
3. John 13.34.
4. Luke 10.27.
5. Luke 11.28.
6. I Corinthians 15.33. See AV and New Revised Standard Version.
7. Charles de Foucauld. 1858–1916. He was eventually killed by Tuareg tribesmen. Two French missionary associations – the Association Charles de Foucauld and the Mission de Foucauld carry on his work.
8. From F.P. Harton, *The Elements of the Spiritual life*. SPCK. 1950. p. 278.
9. Teresa of Avila. *The Interior Castle*. Halycon Backhouse. 1988. p. 38ff. Teresa was the first to draw attention to the existence of states of prayer between discursive meditation and the summit prayer, at that time called ecstasy. See *The Crucible of Love*. E. W. Trueman Dicken. Darton Longman and Todd. 1963. pp. 107–8 & p. 180.
10. Matthew 6.20.
11. John 20.28.
12. See *Studies in the Fourth Gospel*, edited by F.L. Cross. F.R. Mowbray. 1957. Chapter viii article by G.L. Phillips.
13. Luke 1.38.
14. In *The Grammar of Assent*, Newman made the case for a faculty of judgement which he called the illative sense.
15. The subplot in *The Rivals*, the play by Sheridan, revolves around Faulkland and his love for Julia. He is infuriatingly wracked with doubts about whether she loves him.
16. Luke 19.17.
17. Luke 14.10.

18. Psalm 106.25.
19. Matthew 28.20.
20. Thomas Merton. Trappist monk and well known writer in the second half of the twentieth century.
21. I Samuel 3.9.

Chapter Two

The cock crowed

After his third denial Peter realised the enormity of what he had done. A humbled Peter broke down! Only a few hours after telling Jesus that he would never betray him, he denied that he ever knew him. He could have excused himself on the grounds that he had no choice. He could have counted on the sympathy of the other disciples, because they too had let Jesus down by running away after similar professions of loyalty.[1] Peter was distraught when he realised that he was not nearly as willing to lay down his life as he thought. It was a humbler and wiser man who encountered Jesus. The Gospel records this moving moment in a few words:

"The Lord turned and looked on Peter."[2]

Peter knew the joy of sin forgiven. It was a life-changing moment. It is a very different Peter about whom we read in the Acts of the Apostles: Peter the fearless preacher, Peter healing the sick at the temple gate, Peter in prison, Peter preaching the gospel to the gentile Cornelius.

If, when we have left the royal highway of loving obedience, we express our love for God by working together with him to put matters right, the work of restoration will begin straight away. He will liberate us with the keys of forgiveness and mercy. He will bless us with gifts of wholeness and healing. He will give us the grace and strength to weather all that we might be called to endure, as we set off once more along the straight and narrow way.

Acknowledging our sinfulness, confronting it and dealing with it is one of the first things we have to do, as we set out on the journey of prayer. The amount of work to be done will depend on the state of the heart.

To help us see what needs to be done, we pray that God the Holy Spirit would flood our innermost being with light. When we see what is wrong, we ask for guidance in the work of cleansing and renewal.

The truth will make you free

Two Protestant divines, one garrulous and greedy, the other ascetic, thoughtful and wise, were dining together. They were arguing about whether it was possible to be perfect in this life. To settle the matter the ascetic divine, who knew full well that all have sinned and all have fallen short of the glory of God,[3] opted for a practical experiment. He poured a jug of ice cold water over the head of his garrulous colleague, who had foolishly claimed that he was already perfect. The surprised recipient of this chilling baptism jumped up in a fury and uttered what the captain of the HMS Pinafore called a big, big D.

Once we have become aware of sin and acknowledged our sinfulness, there is no excuse for complacency. St Paul had a tussle with new Christians who had enjoyed the blessings of forgiveness but didn't see why they should change. They had experienced the joy of forgiveness and the spiritual blessings of the convert, but naively believed that they could have the best of both worlds. Why not have a good time, and live our lives exactly as we did before? Why change anything if forgiveness and mercy are free? Why don't we do exactly what we want to do, when we want to do it and then come back for another dose of free forgiveness? "Why not sin," they asked, "that grace may abound?"[4] St Paul's answer: "By no means!"

Sin has consequences. A bad apple corrupts. A small fault bears bad fruit. For example, a cigarette thrown idly out of a car window could ignite a forest fire which might cause damage or loss. Leaving the fork in the hay might cause serious injury. Although forgiveness takes a load off our backs, it cannot eliminate all the damage done. For example, if we are thoughtless, unkind or casual about what we say, we might consider our fault trivial and justify ourselves on the grounds that we have only spoken our mind. Comfortably cocooned in self-righteous complacency, we fail to notice the way a small wound inflicted upon another by the kiss of a poisonous word might putrefy, and we may remain culpably ignorant of the way the infection of poisonous words can spread.

In the same way that hearing is deadened by deafening music or the guns on the rifle range, so our consciences will atrophy if we fail to make a sincere effort to listen to God and amend our lives.

The two sons

The prodigal son[5] was deaf to the words of his father and blind to the potentially rotten fruit of his own blinkered behaviour. I doubt if it crossed his mind that his actions might have negative consequences. However, life in the pigpen became God's opportunity to turn him around. Contrast the pride of the prodigal who left home with his head in the air, with the humility displayed by the penitent as he prepared to kneel before his father and cry out, "Father I have sinned against heaven and before thee and am no more worthy to be called thy son."[6] Foolish pride, which had caused the prodigal to strut out of his father's house like a peacock, was tossed into the furnace of love and recast as humility.

17

Meanwhile, the older brother's heart froze solid. He declined his father's invitation to the party because he was too proud to let go of his resentment. The possibility of weeping over his own poor soul was off the radar. He was preoccupied with his own feelings and saw nothing wrong with his stubbornness. It never crossed his mind that he was being self righteous. He experienced the peace of the complacent. This is not the peace of the forgiven, but the peace of a man whose conscience has a malfunction; the false peace of a man who has a whimpering dormouse for a conscience. "Me, me, me" consumed him! "I haven't done anything wrong; it's my little brother who has upset the applecart and disgraced the family. Can't you see why I am so cross and upset? I'm not spoiling any party. I can't possibly imagine why you think it's my fault. It's all the fault of that silly little brother of mine who foolishly wasted all the family money on loose living, squandered our inheritance and made life a misery for us all."

The father

As we continue to ponder this parable, our attention moves from the two sons to the father. In him we see a model of the kind of love which we long to see take root in our own hearts. We are deeply moved by his indestructible love. No doubt the father drew attention to the flaws in the prodigal's dotty schemes; and yet when he had done all he could to dissuade him from his folly, he allowed him to set off on his journey, fearing that he would end up in trouble but hoping that all would be well.

What wisdom and courage we see in the willingness of the father to let go of his son! What patience we see as he yearned for his return! What faith, hope and love we see as he stood and waited! Consider the father's pain as he explained to his older son why they were having a party: "This, your brother, was dead and is alive again, was lost and is found."[7]

All have sinned

During my ministry, I came across people who were irritated by what they considered to be the injustice done to the older brother who stayed at home and continued to work on the farm. They took his side, claiming that he had done nothing wrong and was entitled to be angry, bitter and resentful.

I also saw the confusion and puzzlement of prodigals who had experienced the love and mercy of God, when they saw that their brothers and sisters in Christ didn't cheerfully accept the invitation to the party to celebrate their return!

When I preached on the text, "All have sinned, and all have fallen short of the glory of God,"[8] I could see that a raw nerve was touched. People looked around wondering who the sinner was! Faithful church people thought these words couldn't possibly apply to them. Prickly self-righteous thoughts sparked, spluttered and crackled with irritation. Quoting this text was like putting a silver spoon in the microwave.

It's easy for new Christians to mistake the blessing and peace of forgiveness as a sign that they have made it, that because sin has been washed away they are already perfect. It is true that those who have taken the first step in Gospel living enter the joy and peace of believing, but we don't have to look further than the Sermon on the Mount to see that there is still much to be done. We haven't made it. We've hardly started.

Maybe we are concerned that if we say we are sinners, people will think that we are admitting to being monsters. Nevertheless, if we refuse to face the truth that all have sinned, even though some sins are much worse than others, our souls will remain incarcerated in the jailhouse of pride. If we are not prepared to look at our failings and take steps to put things right, how will we ever make any spiritual progress?

Only a man numbed by pride would feel uncomfortable about

being in the same boat as Paul who persecuted Christians, Peter who denied Jesus, and the disciples who ran away at the first sign of serious trouble. The people of God are all forgiven sinners. The humiliation and pain of acknowledging our sin bears no comparison with the joy of sin forgiven.

The prodigal saw that he had gone astray and did something about it. The older brother was self righteous and didn't. He was so preoccupied with his brother's failings that he couldn't see his own.

Jesus said, "Judge not that ye be not judged."[9]

It was Gilbert of Sempringham who penned the memorable lines,

> "Hypocrisy the meanest sin,
> All fair without and foul within."[10]

And it was the words on the tombstone of the legendary Digswell poacher Kitty Nash which often caught my eye as I walked reflectively around the churchyard:

> "Not the righteous, not the righteous – sinners Jesus came to call."[11]

The enemy

Although we are responsible for our own actions, we can't ignore the shenanigans of the enemy. The experiences of Jesus in his forty days in the wilderness were real and challenging.

Can anyone who has seen film clips of tyrants working the crowds doubt that there is more to evil than human peccadilloes? Can anyone who has read about and understood the way that ordinary men and women can be mesmerized and ensnared by the monstrosities of evil regimes think for a moment that the forces of evil don't exist?

In prayer, fasting and the conduct of our lives, we do our best to keep clear of the forces of evil so that we aren't compromised. Evil is dangerous. We don't play with fire. Nevertheless, the fact that care is required in all that we think, say or do, need no more alarm us than the requirement to wash our hands before preparing food or looking both ways before we cross the road.

"Be sober, be vigilant," we are reminded in the service of Compline.

"Your adversary the devil as a roaring lion seeketh whom he may devour, whom resist steadfast in the faith."[12]

Although Satan opposes God's work, we shouldn't forget that in Christ Jesus the battle is won.

I was schooled in country wisdom which taught respect for animals. I understood that farm animals were not virtual realities promoting the joys of eating butter but had minds and wills of their own. If an animal was aggressive, we were advised to stay away and keep calm. It was better to walk quietly away rather than playing the foolish hero. In the same way it is unwise to make a lot of fuss and palaver when we are confronted by evil. It is better to be unruffled and put our trust in God.

The Lord's Prayer

When we are disturbed by the powers of darkness, we turn to the familiar words of the Lord's Prayer, "Deliver us from evil."

Simply with a mustard seed of faith, we ask God to protect us from the wiles of Satan. Because actions speak louder than words, it is good to make the sign of the Cross. If we feel that the adversary is making mischief, we pray that Jesus Christ would bind him and all his pea-brained minions. Our prayer might be a straightforward request using such words as, "Lord Jesus Christ, bind all that is evil, all that is not of you, and protect us in our hour of need."

Once we have renounced Satan, we turn our backs on him to face Christ, in whom we believe and trust. In this way we are on firm ground and in the right place to deal with trouble. To help us to focus on God, we lift up our hearts in praise, while giving thanks that Jesus Christ is Lord of heaven and Lord of earth and Lord of all that ever shall be.

When put to the test, we put on the whole armour of God which includes the helmet of salvation, the breastplate of righteousness, the girdle of truth, the sword of the Spirit and the gospel of peace.[13]

Exorcism

Exorcism is casting out the Satanic when in occupation. It is a special gift which must be confirmed by the appropriate Church authorities. Although exorcists in the early Church were among the minor orders, generally speaking they weren't ordained, because exorcism is a charism rather than an office. We should never dabble in this territory unless our ministry has been approved. Exorcism is a specialist function like that of the brave young men and women who are trained and skilled in bomb disposal.

Self-examination

Some souls are as insensitive as an elephant's hide, while others are as tender as gossamer. There is a difference between those whose consciences are dead and need an army of picadors to arouse them and sensitive souls who take the words, "Do no sinful action," to mean that it's unsafe to get out of bed in the morning. To further complicate matters, some who are hyper-sensitive about the sins of the flesh are blind to the presence of the more serious and well-concealed sins of pride and hypocrisy.

In order to see our sin, we humble ourselves, empty our minds of everything and pray that we might see what is of concern to God.

Guided by the Holy Spirit, we review what needs to be done. Eating too many chocolates or being crotchety and ragged round the edges may not be as serious as pride, envy, doubt, fear and sloth. So long as we are attentive, what we can't see in fifteen minutes is best left for another day. Although over-zealous scrabbling around looking for the minutiae is often pride masquerading as humility, the little sins shouldn't be swept under the carpet.

It isn't good to embark upon searching self-examination unless we are secure in the love and mercy of God. If we go on a trawl for sin without acknowledging the wideness of God's mercy, we might find ourselves wallowing in self pity.

In the Dialogue of Catherine of Sienna[14] we read,

"I do not wish the soul to consider her sins either in general, or in particular, without also remembering the broadness of his mercy, for fear that otherwise she might be brought to confusion."

We'll never see the full extent of the homework to be done until the light of the Holy Spirit shines in the deepest recesses of the soul. It isn't because all is well that we are untroubled, but because we have no idea what is going on and we find it uncongenial to think of ourselves as sinners. Until such a time as the veil is removed and we see that we are sinners, whenever the preacher says for the umpteenth time, "All have sinned, all have fallen short of the glory of God,"[15] we look around anxiously wondering where the sinner is!

When the Holy Spirit illuminates the soul, we begin to see that we are not wholly unlike the curmudgeonly older brother in the parable. There is just a tinge of envy whenever a party is given for someone else, a tad of bitterness when the little brother seems to have got away with it. Maybe we are resentful and angry when we have to do all the work, while others seem to have an easy ride.

We certainly don't consider ourselves to be anything like the prodigal. But isn't there just a smidgen of jealousy when we see a notorious sinner forgiven and get off scot free? In a small corner of our heart of hearts, don't we want to see him grovel and pay the full tariff for his crimes? And as we consider his failings, isn't there just a little smirk as we smugly reassure ourselves that a leopard will never change its spots?

The prodigal, we like to believe, is beyond the pale. We would never be so stupid. We would never be so rebellious. We would never be so insensitive. We would never treat our family like that. We aren't arrogant, thoughtless, greedy or promiscuous, and when did we ever go on the razzle or waste our lives in riotous living?

It's only possible to bask in such glorious self righteous folly if we aren't in touch with the true state of our own soul and acknowledge the simple truth: "There but for the grace of God go I."

The shoe on the roof

Not long ago, a little girl was standing outside my cottage with tears streaming down her cheeks. When asked what was the matter, she told me that she had lost her shoe on the roof. When asked how it got there, she peered through moistened eyes and said, "I was just putting on my shoe."

How could she have thought that her fanciful story was believable? And why hadn't she told us what really happened? Was she frightened of getting into trouble with her mother, or reluctant to tell tales about the little boy who had just disappeared round the corner?

Our refusal to face the facts about what is going on in the

fallen part of our human nature and the way that we so readily spin a yarn in our own favour, comes from a similar place of insecurity as the imaginative account of the little girl. We weave cunning narratives in our minds to demonstrate that we are in the right, because we don't want to see that we are not as righteous as we like to believe.

Most of us are not so unlike the prodigal in our feeble efforts to deal with pride or the sins of the flesh, and we are little better than the older brother in dealing with hatred and envy, but it is good to remember that we can only really face up to the vexed question of sin if we are secure in the knowledge that "there is more joy in heaven over one sinner who repents, than over ninety and nine just persons who need no repentance."[16]

A forgiving heart

Amongst the virtues, there is one which is seldom taken sufficiently seriously. A forgiving heart isn't a soft option. Unconditional Christian forgiveness is only achievable because in the long run God sorts everything out. Unconditional forgiveness is only possible if we trust him who overcomes evil with good. Further, we are required to forgive not once, but again and again – "Not until seven times, but until seventy times seven."[17]

It isn't easy to forgive and forget, to wipe the slate completely clean so that we harbour no bitterness or resentment, when we are the victims of injustice or hatred; but we aren't alone. God helps us to be merciful and forgiving by an infusion of his love, which will strengthen and help us in our resolve to walk the way of the Cross.

The truth of the centrality of forgiveness was emblazoned on the Cross, when Jesus said, "Father forgive them for they know not what they do."[18] When we have been unjustly wronged and we lie awake at night jangling with all kinds of emotions, our minds go round and round in circles feeding on our sense of injustice and pain. Although it is important to face up to the existence of feelings of resentment, they are not to be indulged but challenged. Those who experience such moments know only too well how hard it is to live out the injunction of St Paul, "Be angry and sin not."[19]

But when we turn to the Gospel for help we find that the message is perfectly clear: Forgive, forgive, and forgive again. The Cross shows us the way. We forgive unconditionally. We don't wait until there has been a formal apology or ample restitution. We take a risk. We forgive because forgiveness is the way of Christ.

Those who want to celebrate the joy of sin forgiven must accept that our freedom to bathe in the cleansing waters of forgiveness will be impaired if we are unwilling to forgive those who have wronged us. We don't have to look beyond the Lord's Prayer to see that a necessary preparation for receiving forgiveness is to follow Jesus in our willingness to forgive others.

The joy of sin forgiven

Over many years I have witnessed and experienced the joy of sin forgiven in sacramental confession. I have seen the joy and freedom of sin forgiven in charismatic worship. I have seen people delivered from their chains in pastoral interviews and services of healing. I have celebrated the release of captive souls. I know people who have found the joy of sin forgiven in the secret place or kneeling by their bedside. I have witnessed people dancing for joy when their burden is lifted. I have danced for joy myself in great Anglican cathedrals.

Peter knew that he had failed to live up to his own high expectations. I imagine it was not just the betrayal that troubled him, but also the pride which had tricked him into making the glib assurance that he would follow Jesus all the way to the Cross. But

26

in a single moment the slate was wiped clean. A humble and contrite Peter met the merciful gaze of Jesus – a moment summed up succinctly in the Gospel with the words, "The Lord looked on Peter."[20]

Notes

1. Mark 14. 50.
2. Luke 22.61.
3. Romans 3.23.
4. Romans 6.1ff.
5. Luke 15.11ff.
6. Luke 15.21.
7. Luke 15.32.
8. See note 3 above.
9. Matthew 7.1.
10. Gilbert of Sempringham. 1083–1189!! Founder of the Gilbertines in Sempringham in Lincolnshire. Founded the only purely English order with seven women. At his death there were nine double monasteries, and four for canons.
11. Matthew 9.13.
12. Words from the service of Compline, taken from 1 Peter 5.8.
13. Ephesians 6.11. I have not followed St Paul's order.
14. St Catherine of Sienna circa 1347–1380. Dominican tertiary. Visionary who became involved in Church politics at the highest level. See Mysticism. Evelyn Underhill p. 200ff.
15. See note 3 above.
16. Luke 15.7.
17. Matthew 18.22.
18. Luke 23.34.
19. Ephesians 4.26.
20. See note 2 above.

Chapter Three

My sheep know my voice

Callings and vocations

"There are callings in this church tonight," announced the prophetic voice of a visiting speaker.[1] The minister wasn't only referring to the church's ordained ministry. Callings might include a call to prayer or to any one of a variety of different forms of service.

To ensure that a calling continues to be a response to the loving purposes of God, and to steer clear of what I call the "me and my ministry" problem, it is essential that it stays grounded in humility. The young Isaiah didn't say, "Great! When do I start?" He cried out, "I am a man of unclean lips and dwell amidst a people of unclean lips."[2]

A calling might be revealed internally in a dream, vision, locution, hunch or inspiration, or it might be identified and encouraged by others. If we are called to a public ministry, it should in due course be confirmed by the wider Christian community.

Another way we discover vocation is experimental. This might be compared with the search for Tigger's breakfast in the story by A.A. Milne. Tigger assured his companions that he liked everything. So he was taken to see Piglet, who offered him acorns which he hated and then to Eeyore, who shared his thistles which he loathed. Just as they began to think that their search for breakfast had failed, he tasted Roo's amazing extract of malt, about which he was ecstatic.

If in our heart of hearts we feel there is something we are called to do, but don't know what it is, a vocation might be unearthed by the process of elimination. This has been likened to being in a circular room with many doors. All the doors are closed but only one is unlocked. As we have no keys, the only way to find the unlocked door is to try all the handles until we find the door which opens.

God's proposals

Responding to callings is seconding God's proposals. The first kind of proposal includes things we are required to do because we are who we are, and we are where we are. What God requires of us is determined by our situation. If we are not prevented for an outstandingly good reason, it behoves us to get up in the morning, go to work, do the shopping, look after the family and put out the rubbish. We are also commanded to love God and our neighbour, who is more likely to be found next door than sitting on a polar ice cap. The will of God signified includes all our natural responsibilities. These are not bleak and barren duties, but opportunities to do little things with great love.

The second kind of proposal is concerned with God's special assignments. If we listen to the voice of the Good Shepherd these will be revealed. The disciples were called to leave their nets to become fishers of men.[3] The Priest and the Levite were so preoccupied with the daily round and the common task that they failed to respond to the call to tend the man mugged by robbers on the rocky Jericho road.[4]

Sealed orders

In a sermon Peter Marshall, a former chaplain to the Senate in the U.S.A., described God's special assignments as sealed orders.[5]

We are presented with secret instructions like military orders, in which God indicates what he wants us to do. Opening our sealed orders is prayerful listening. The more attentively we listen, the more receptive we become to our orders and the more opportunities we find to second them.

God is God. He never went away and he never will. He speaks to us as surely as he spoke to Abraham, Isaac and Jacob. He spoke to Isaiah in the temple and awoke the child Samuel with a message for Eli the priest. Throughout the Scriptures God speaks to men, women and children. If we can't, won't or don't hear the voice of God, or if we aren't sure what he is saying, we take heart from the teaching of Père de Caussade,[6] who noted that to put us back on track, God will get behind us and give us a push.

Should we be unsure of what is required of us, we have no alternative but to do the best we can – that is to set out on a chosen course, while trusting that God will correct us if we go wrong. God alone is good. God alone knows what's best for us. Should a course of action fit in too cosily with our own wants and preferences, it is wise to pause and reconsider. In such a situation, we take even more care in discerning what is truly of God. It might not be what we want.[7]

If the blackboard of the mind is packed with our own inclinations and desires, it won't be easy to discern what God is saying until we wipe it clean. If it is our heart's desire to do God's will, we set aside our own inclinations. For example, if we ignore our sealed orders we might assume that we must go to a family gathering. If on the other hand, we search for our sealed orders and study them carefully, we might discover that God has other plans.

The voice of the Good Shepherd

Once we have settled in the secret place and have set aside our own preferences, inclinations and desires, we listen closely as we try to hear what God is saying.

As a parish priest, my own daily practice was to keep a running list of things to be done, which were crossed off when completed. Once a day I would wait upon the Lord, empty my mind of my own presuppositions and listen. Prayerfully I would consider each item on my list. Certain things stood out. It is difficult to explain, but amongst the things that I might be doing, some came to the surface. They required immediate attention. Things on my list which I had overlooked popped up. Things which I hadn't even considered would come to mind. Thoughts, intimations, intuitions, hunches or words surfaced, which could be tested by the normal processes of reasonable discernment.[8]

Events

God speaks to us through events. Teresa of Avila wrote, "Do not suppose that because we cannot hear him he is silent."[9]

St Theresa of Lisieux said, "Though I have never heard him speak, I know he is with me, always guiding me – as a rule not in prayer but in the midst of daily tasks."[10]

Dreams

God also speaks through dreams. St Paul dreamt that a man of Macedonia was calling.[11] He had already made plans for the following day, but acknowledged that his dream conveyed a communication from God. He changed his route and set off for Macedonia to preach the Gospel.

Blocks

Although human reason plays an important role in discernment, our ability to hear what God is saying will be hampered if we pay no heed to the words of the epistle of St James, "If the Lord wills, we shall do this or that."[12] If we close our ears to God we soon go off track.

Sloth and apathy also prevent us from hearing what God is saying and so too do bright ideas of our own devising. Sudden inspirations, which we mistakenly think are from God, give themselves away by being driven, demanding, and over excitable. They quickly fade and never bear fruit that lasts. Beware! They often follow hard on the heels of a genuine inspiration of the Holy Spirit.

Communications laced with anxiety are also seriously suspect. As often as not, they are the product of our fear and we do well to disregard them. Last of all, it is good to remember that the Holy Spirit leads but the devil drives.

Discernment

John Henry Newman described the illative sense as an intuitive adjudicator. It is a faculty which assists us in making sound judgements through a process of inference, which leads to working certainties. It functions like a jury in a court of law. We study evidence as it is placed before us and, by inserting the pieces of the jigsaw puzzle, we gradually begin to see the true picture. As the picture forms, we alight upon working certainties. In this way, the illative sense enables us to step out in faith, rather than forever holding back.[13]

Gifts of discernment are natural gifts charged with the Holy Spirit. Spiritual discernment is looking at the same realities with the same pair of eyes but with a different pair of glasses. Spiritual seeing is seeing another dimension of the same reality. One person sees a middle-aged woman nursing a sick relative. Another sees a saint. The Holy Spirit helps us to see further and deeper than the natural eye, to see with the eye of the soul.

For a little while, St Theresa of Lisieux was preoccupied with an honourable desire to serve God as a nurse or a missionary. It was in a moment of disclosure that she realised that her vocation was much simpler. She was called to stay put and minister to those whom God sent. Because her heart was centred on God, she realised that her vocation was to set aside her ambitions and to love her carers and visitors. Her sealed orders sprung a surprise. Without going anywhere, her vocation was a call to a complete volte-face. It was simple. She was to love her neighbours, and her neighbours were there before her very eyes. They were the elderly sisters who looked after her and those who came to her sick room. When she saw this she exclaimed, "O Jesus my love, my vocation is found at last: my vocation is to love."[14]

Help

There are three main aids to discernment:

1. The Bible and Christian teaching
2. The experience of the saints
3. Personal inspiration

The Bible is much more than a map. Christian writings are more than manuals of instruction. The Bible is not a little red book which must be slavishly followed; it is a work of art in which we see the image of God, who is love, revealed in his son Jesus Christ by the power of the Holy Spirit. It is a picture on a perishable canvas made of earthly pigment, in which the eye of faith can discern the loving presence and activity of God in a fallen world.

In the Bible we learn that not even Moses or David were

plaster cast saints,[15] but the God of Abraham, Isaac and Jacob was indeed the living God. Although practical questions arise for which the words of the Bible have no definitive answers, it makes known the one who is the answer. Those who try to reduce the Bible to an ethical code fail to acknowledge that Christ is the Word of God. Without the doctrine the Christian ethic fails. Christ is the message. Although the Sermon on the Mount contains clear teaching, it doesn't give a blow-by-blow account of exactly how we may "love one another as I have loved you."[16]

The message of the Bible is that the nearer we draw to Christ, the more we behold him, the more the Holy Spirit will help us to love, honour and serve him.[17]

It can hardly be denied that a remarkable indication of the truth of the Gospel is the rapprochement between what Jesus said and what he did. He did what he commanded us to do and all that he did was in accordance with the Father's will. For example Jesus said, "Greater love hath no man than this, that a man lay down his life for his friends."[18] So this is what he did. As the eye of the soul blinks and becomes accustomed to the light of day, we see for ourselves that "Truly this man is the son of God."[19]

From Jesus we learn that we are called to love, not to hate, to be merciful, not to seek revenge, to be patient, not to be angry, to die to selfish desires and to rejoice when we are persecuted. The Bible is the Moses basket in which we discover Jesus Christ the living Word, the giver of the new commandment and the fount of all that is good.

Christian teaching is accumulated wisdom rooted in prayer and grounded in love. Authentic Christian theology is more than knowing about God; it is the fruit of knowing God in the intimacy of the soul.

In a remarkable account of the practice of a great scholar who was both a theologian and a contemplative, Brother Reginald described the way that St Thomas Aquinas immersed himself in prayer as he prepared himself for writing:

> "My brothers, while he was still in this life my master (the angelic doctor) forbade me to disclose the admirable things concerning him whereof I had been witness. One of these things was that he had acquired his science not by human industry, but by the merit of prayer, for whenever he wished to study, discuss, read, write or dictate, he first had recourse to prayer in private and poured forth his soul with tears in order to discover the divine secrets, and by the merits of this prayer his doubts were removed, and he issued therefrom fully instructed."[20]

The practice of Thomas Aquinas suggests that he didn't consider that the intellect trumped the spiritual. Prayer enables us to see more clearly and to think without prejudice. Belief is not contrary to reason. Yet seeing with the eye of the soul takes us beyond reason, for there is more to the mental life than the exercise of the little grey cells. Jesus said, "Who of you by taking thought can add a cubit to his stature?"[21]

Angels and messengers

The supernatural world is a mystery beyond our understanding but the Bible is full of angels and angelic communications. The Greek word for angel means a messenger, human or divine.

Shortly after I had a mini stroke, I was faced with the task of trying to move a broken-down car from the main road, up a short steep slope, to the garage. It was dusk and there was no one in sight to help me. I stood there thinking to myself, "I really shouldn't be doing this." I had just offered up an unspoken help prayer, when a young man appeared beside me. He came from nowhere. Moments later, I was alone at the top of the slope, standing by the car. My hand was still resting on the back but I hadn't pushed it. When I looked around, there was no one there. Not a little surprised, I ran down the slope and looked left and right. There was a clear view, and not a soul in sight. There were no other cars or people in the vicinity at any time either before or after the incident. Although my helper appeared to be a young man, there was an extraordinary grace about him. I have no doubt that I was given divine assistance but who was my helper?

Spotting what comes from where

There is nothing which comes from the mind which hasn't been humanly processed. Every communication and inspiration, from whatever source, human or divine, is interpreted by a fallible mind and uttered and expressed in imperfect language and images. Nevertheless, so long as our heart is in the right place, we shouldn't hesitate to leave the starting blocks because we are frightened of making mistakes or worried about getting it wrong.

We seek for illumination by holding up our intimations to the light of God's love. With practice, we become more adept at spotting what comes from where. This doesn't mean that little things don't matter. Remember the butterfly effect.[22] Little things do matter. The Gospel recalls the words of Jesus in the parable of the talents:

> "Well done, thou good and faithful servant: thou hast been faithful over a few things. I will make thee ruler over many things. Enter thou into the joy of thy Lord."[23]

Those who are faithful in little things will be entrusted with greater.

God speaks to you and me

One day I set out to mow the lawn. I was irritated because I was busy and had a sermon to prepare. I knew that the grass couldn't wait till the afternoon. Because of his reaction to grass, I had to down tools long before my asthmatic son came home from school. I marched up and down the lawn for a while before being stopped in my tracks by an intuition: "Now, in this garden, pushing and pulling this mowing machine is where God wants me to be."

It was as if God said, "If I ask you to mow the grass, trust me about time for parish and family, because this precious time is also a time for solitude and prayer."

God speaks to us about little matters. If in Lent we forget that we have decided to give up drinking tea or coffee, a gentle intimation might serve as a reminder. Should we have forgotten an appointment, we might find ourselves in the right place at the right time. If we are spiritually alert, we will be receptive to little hints and clear clues about what we are called to do and when and how to do it.

When we are unsure we carry on by making the best decisions we can, confident that if it is our underlying desire to do the will of God and we unwittingly go off track, we will be guided back with a gentle nudge.

In little matters simple tests suffice. Prayerfully we try to assess whether what has come to mind is good and of God. At the natural level we apply common sense.

Should we receive an intimation that we are to wash the bathroom floor, we check to see if it witnesses to the spirit, feels right and is a sensible decision. It is a waste of time to spend half an hour worrying about what to do. It is better to go straight to the cleaning cupboard, get out the mop and bucket and set to work. If the intimation is of God we won't lose our peace as we scrub the bathroom floor and we might discover that there was a very good reason why God set this particular task at this particular time. Perhaps the lost coin is lying hidden under the clothes basket!

God is the source of the natural and the spiritual. What matters is not our ability to disentangle them in order to see where one ends and the other begins, but being able to discern what is in accordance with the loving purposes of God, so that we can second his proposals.

A natural thought might be inspired by God. An exciting spiritual notion might come from the recesses of the human mind. For this reason inspirations should always be checked. In important matters we take time, look for confirmations and apply all the tools of discernment. In lesser matters we make a quick and decisive judgement. It is not a question of the spiritual being good and the natural bad, but whether we are seconding God's proposals.

Seeing through a glass darkly

Recently I visited the dentist. He told me that I had an abscess which had spread north, south, east and west. I was not surprised because I looked like a prize fighter. I made a further appointment so that he could deal with the matter. After an hour of drilling and digging, he told me that he had done his best but still hadn't been able to remove all the debris. So it is with self-deception. We may never get rid of it all but the more we clear away, the less likely we are to be tripped up.

When we say that a communication is of God, we are not denying that it is interpreted by our fallible human minds, but acknowledging that with the help of God it's possible to identify, comprehend and second his proposals.

Confirmations

Although in little matters we may make quick decisions, in more important ones we look for confirmations.

Twenty years ago a church member had a vision. It was about a small party from St John's Church. She saw suitcases filled with summer clothes in Caribbean style and a variety of different items together with the words, "My peace will go with you on the journey."[24] She had no idea what it meant, but in the event there were three confirmations. The Canon Missioner invited a group from St John's Church to visit Guyana to assist in the Sharing of Ministries Abroad. The three people invited to make the journey each felt that this was a call of God and, within a few days, the Church community provided the £1,500 required for the air fares.

In April 1990 we travelled to Georgetown. The fruit of the visit is still seen over twenty years and three visits later. We retain prayer links with the Church in Guyana and people there join us in daily watches of prayer.

Timing

Timing is all important. To do the right thing at the wrong time is to do the wrong thing. Teresa of Avila sought a confirmation from her confessor about a further development. She felt sure that the community was to open a house in a certain town. She deferred to her confessor, who considered that she was mistaken. Teresa put the matter on one side and waited. A while later the house was acquired. Her willingness to be humble and patient was vindicated. She was right about the house. Was her confessor right about the timing?

In our prayers we don't try to change the mind of God, but to align ourselves with his will. We are not asking him to move pieces around on a giant chessboard but petitioning him to help us to be where he wants us to be. Nothing is too small for God. In sharing our most intimate concerns with him, we are left in no doubt that he is love.

39

Treasures old and new

A kind of autopilot safely guides those who are immersed in prayer through the complexities of life, while drawing upon treasures old and new. Material stored away in the hidden recesses of the human psyche comes to the surface and illuminates our daily lives. A word of scripture or a word of wisdom emerges at just the right moment. A line from a well-known hymn or spiritual song sheds light on the present, by illuminating it with precious teaching material stored away in the past. The kaleidoscope is shaken. Bits and pieces form a remarkable new pattern which conveys a brand new message.

Let me explain with a cricketing analogy. It is obvious that a batsman who faces a ball hurtling down at a hundred miles an hour doesn't have time to make a precise calculation of when it will hit him on the head and floor him or disappear over the pavilion for six. The mind goes into autopilot. It has been pre-programmed. Quite how is a mystery, but in the split second that the ball hurtles down the pitch, he will be in trouble if he hesitates to do some mental arithmetic. The greatest batsmen are particularly blessed with such an instinctive and intuitive gift.

By analogy, the same is true in our spiritual lives. The more we pray, meditate and contemplate, the more we are spiritually fed, the more such an underground spiritual resource develops and operates. We mysteriously find ourselves in the right place at the right time and about God's business, but might have little idea how we came to be there. Although unaware that God has given us a push, we see his hand in the outcome.

The more we attend to our sealed orders in times set aside for prayer, the more receptive we will be as he communicates during the course of the day. Panic pleas are replaced by a deep and enduring trust. We no longer waste time telling God what we want, but attend to our sealed orders. We see the next step not just by applying common sense or meditating upon the Gospel but by prayerfully living the sacrament of the present moment.[25]

God communicates at any time. God uses every means of communication. The word of God might be a word of scripture. The word of God might be a word of wisdom. The word of God might be revealed in a dream, vision or locution. The word of God might be a spiritual inspiration, intuition or hunch. God will speak to us in all these ways. And of course, he will speak to us through events.

At all times it is good to keep a close watch to see if a communication reflects the teachings of the Gospel, which reveal the mind of Christ and witness to the human spirit. There is much to be learned from humbly evaluating the fruits of our labours, to see if they are good and of God. It is also good to look within, to see whether the soul is blessed with the trademark traces of love, joy and peace.

Sealed orders are communicated from God the Father, through the Son, in the power of the Holy Spirit. Our sealed orders are concerned with the small part we are called to play in building the kingdom of Christ. If we try to travel any other way than the way of Christ, we risk losing sight of the miracle of the incarnation, in which God chose not to reject our human nature but to redeem it.

Our Lord didn't say that no-one would ever hear his voice again once we had the Bible. Our Lord didn't say that because the Holy Spirit fell upon the disciples at Pentecost, he would retire. Our Lord didn't say that because he spoke to the prophets and revealed himself in his Son, the line would go dead. He simply said,

"My sheep know my voice."[26]

Notes

1. The Revd Jean Darnell, a Pentecostal minister.
2. Isaiah 6.1–6.
3. Mark 1.16ff.

4. Luke 10.29ff.
5. I think it was in a collection of sermons in the book entitled, *A man called Peter.*
6. Père de Caussade. A Jesuit priest who played an important part in encouraging contemplative prayer at a time when many were nervous about Quietism.
7. St John of the Cross. Prologue to the Ascent. A.T. Nicolas. Samuel Weiser Inc. 1996. p.161. For we are not writing here on moral and pleasing subjects addressed to the type of spiritual person who likes to reach God by tasting sweet and pleasing things. We are dealing with a substantial and solid doctrine applicable to everyone who wishes to reach the nakedness of the spirit about which I am writing.
8. See Appendix.
9. St Teresa of Avila. See Chapter One note 9.
10. St Theresa of Lisieux. *The Little Flower of Jesus.* Burns Oates and Washbourne. 1944. p. 203.
11. Acts 16.9.
12. James 4.15.
13. See *The Grammar of Assent.* Image books. Doubleday and Co. New York. 1955. One cannot base a guide for life on probabilities and inferences, because life is not long enough to judge them reliably. Life (Newman declared) is for action. To act you must assume and that assumption is called faith (from *The Times* leader 13.9.10.)
14. See note 10 above.
15. Moses killed a man, David had Uriah killed and Jacob cheated on his brother.
16. John 15.12.
17. John 16.13.
18. John 15.13.
19. Matthew 27.54.
20. F.P. Harton. *The elements of the spiritual life.* SPCK. London. 1932. p. 35.
21. Matthew 6.27.
22. The butterfly effect is the notion that a butterfly flapping its wings in Rio de Janeiro can affect the weather in Chicago.
23. Matthew 25.21.
24. *The Best is Yet to Come.* David Thompson. p. 56ff.
25. The Sacrament of the Present Moment. Père de Caussade encouraged his hearers to discern the activity of God in every present moment and to join in, without being discouraged by the past, or fearful about the future.
26. John 10.1–16.

Chapter Four

Loving ourselves for the sake of God

A gasp rippled round the Church like a Mexican wave when the visiting speaker, a priest, said, "I look in the mirror every morning and thank God for making me so beautiful."

The priest wasn't boasting about his transformation by cosmetic surgery or a miracle cure for baldness. He was giving thanks that he was made in the image of God. He who was but a tiny jewel on the ocean floor was praising God for the wonder of his works.

We often find it difficult to love ourselves because we are confounded by the values of secular fashion, which drip-feed us with the notion that beauty is only skin deep. Once we lose the simplicity of a child, many of us fail to see that we are beautiful or we think it arrogant or antisocial to say so. In order to see the true beauty of God as we behold our reflection in the mirror, in order to see beyond a colour supplement image, we must be clothed in humility.

When Jesus said that it was good to be like a child,[1] he wasn't of course saying that we should be like Peter Pan and never grow up, but advising us to retain a childlike disposition of simplicity and trust.

Spiritual difficulties arise because, when we lose the simple trust of a babe in its mother's arms, our faith becomes laced with fear and doubt. We begin to worry about our image and identity. We never sow because we watch the sky; we never reap because we watch the clouds; and sometimes we are as ungrateful as the miserable old woman in the children's tale, who lived in a vinegar bottle but was still grumpy when she moved into a castle.

The ladder of love

St Bernard of Clairvaux[2] portrays the spiritual journey as a ladder of love.

The bottom rung is loving ourselves for our own sake. Need we look further than a toddler having a tantrum to be reminded of this simple truth?

The second step is loving God for our own sake. On this step we move beyond "me, me, me," to being profoundly grateful for the love, mercy and generosity of God. No longer wholly preoccupied with our own demands and desires, we gladly give thanks to God for his goodness and the wonders that he does for the children of men. We love God because he provides. We love God because he first loved us.

The third step is loving God for his sake. This is altruism. Our motives for loving God have been radically purified. Loving God is no longer a response to his continuing provision and many blessings. It is a Copernican moment. The saints on this step have learned that the world doesn't revolve around man, but God.

The fourth step is loving ourselves for the sake of God. For mere mortals this is mind blowing! This is the pinnacle of love. It is doubtful if anyone can reach this place in this mortal life. It is a little death: nothing less than totally, utterly selfless, disinterested love.

God is love

The epistle of St John says, "God is love, and those who live in love live in God, and God lives in them."[3]

As our lives become more Christ-centred, we move up to the second step of the ladder of love. Here we begin to acknowledge that all our instincts and creativity are good and of God. The proclamation that "God saw all that he had made, and behold it was very good," resonates in the soul.

No man hates his own flesh[4]

How can we fail to love ourselves if God our creator loves us? How can we begin to love our neighbour as our own self if we don't love ourselves? God has always loved us and always will. God loved us at the moment of our conception. God loves us when we find ourselves immersed in slurry. God loves us when we come home with our tail between our legs. God even loves us when we harden our hearts and refuse to come to the party. The supreme demonstration of love is to be seen on Calvary, where love broke forth into a loveless world.

If we don't love and own ourselves, we will short change everyone else, for love of self precedes the love of neighbour and is the soil from which it grows.

The priest who stood at the front of the Church and told us that he praised God for making him so beautiful, could see what many miss. He was confident that God created him in his own image and likeness. He understood that in a wonderful and mysterious way he was endowed with the beauty of God.

As we open our hearts in the journey of prayer, the Holy Spirit helps us to see beyond a superficial image. He graciously helps us to see ourselves through the eyes of love. He helps us to see a glimpse of the way we appear in the sight of God. Overcome by this new way of seeing, we put our pride in our pocket and learn a little humility from the children who engagingly sing, "Thank you Lord for making me, me."

The joggers

As I drove around the parish, I saw joggers running around the leafy lanes of Hertfordshire. Some of them called to mind our lack of joy in God's creativity. They looked like pipe cleaner men. Their pallid spindly legs, which hadn't enjoyed the warm embrace of the summer sun, were in danger of slipping down a sluice into the slough of despond, even as their lips breathlessly mumbled the mantra, "No pain, no gain."

Self-hatred is an obstacle to our call to be thankful. It is a bully given permission by pride to taunt us about our inadequacies. The demeanour of the unhappy joggers was like that of false ascetics staggering around, encumbered by a ball and chain. They seemed to be taking pleasure in inflicting self-punishment, rather than taking a proper delight in their poor, unloved bodies.

It is one thing to keep fit, to disperse the toxins or to prepare ourselves for some sporting event: it is quite another to self-harm, take a perverse delight in beating ourselves up or idly dream that we can preserve eternal youth into middle age and beyond. To be in denial about our mortality, and to try to ward it off by pounding the pavements or spending a fortune in the local pharmacy or gym, is to open wide the gates of despair.

We are no more required to earn our place in the love of God, than a newborn babe a place in his mother's affection. If we think that we are only acceptable and loved by God if we get everything right, we will be as miserable as a centipede trying to skip. Dying to self doesn't mean disparaging our creativity, but cutting our ties with the prince of this world, who would like us to have nothing to do with God.

If I really thought that I was just a bunch of molecules wrapped up in a genetic code which emerged from the ether by chance, I don't think I would love myself that much. Because I believe that I am a part of the supreme creativity of God, I love myself a lot. It is not the molecules which excite me, but the ability to love: and as far as I am aware, no one has yet been able to analyse love in a Petri dish.

Over many years in schools and churches, I heard people sing the words of Mrs Alexander's children's hymn[5]:

> All things bright and beautiful,
> The Lord God made them all.

and

> He gave us eyes to see them
> And lips that we might tell
> How great is God almighty.

Before the fall, Adam and Eve loved themselves. So long as they enjoyed the delights of paradise, they were naked and unashamed. But once they had eaten from the forbidden tree, things looked different. They became self-conscious and consumed with guilt.

Whether we see this as the fall, man coming of age, the adolescence of man or even as a fall upwards is immaterial. The truth is that Adam, Eve and the serpent all let the side down. The courts of heaven were unimpressed by the blame game because Adam and Eve were both disobedient, and the serpent did nothing but encourage them. If we refuse to acknowledge our absolute dependence upon God, the central notion around which Friedrich Schleiermacher[6] built his whole theology, we will always be at the mercy of our cultured despisers and will never emerge from beneath our secular carapace.

47

RSVP

The life of the Samaritan woman who encountered Jesus at Jacob's well, was in a mess. She was on her fifth relationship, socially isolated, out of sorts and struggling. The words of Jesus changed her life. He offered her living water, an astonishing outpouring of divine love, while assuring her that, "those who drink from this water will never thirst again."[7]

Such love is available to all, but the poor in spirit will be in a better place to receive it, than the well-heeled, self-sufficient or proud.

In 1874 Father Benson[8] wrote,

"God will sooner work by a simple peasant who gives all the glory to him, for he knows that it is his, than by one of these very clever men who think they are such a gain to any cause that they join."

and

"Distinctions matter very little after death. A corpse after all is but a corpse and we cannot be living to God unless we be as corpses in the world, dead to our old selves."

Mortification

To help us to take up our position in the lowest place, we deal with the murmurs of self-will. Dying to self, or mortification, is the discipline which helps us to grow up. Mortification is the struggle of the emerging butterfly as she fights her way out of the chrysalis because her clothing of self-centredness has become too tight. As she emerges, she prepares to hang on to whatever props God has provided, before drying her wings and fluttering into a clear blue sky.

Mortification is taking up our cross daily. Jesus said, "Whoever does not take up his cross and follow me is not worthy of me," and "Those who find their life will lose it, and those who lose their life for my sake will find it."⁹

Prayer is wriggling out of the grave clothes of sin, so that we are free to spread our wings and prepare to fly.

Taking off

Where do we begin? We practise self-denial by finding time to pray. We focus on God and say a few set prayers or meditate. We use words of our own. We are silent and come to with a start, as we realise the mind has gone AWOL. We are distracted by something in the wrong place on the mantelpiece or begin to think about the coming day. Our worry list surfaces. We anxiously look at the clock and see that time has stood still.

Keeping our focus is like taking an undisciplined dog for a walk in the woods. We have hardly set out when off it scampers and is soon out of sight. We run around whistling and calling. After a while it comes racing back, panting, wagging its tail and looking very pleased with itself. Before we can fix the lead it's off again. Worse still, like a golden retriever, it takes a muddy dip, rolls in stagnant pools and needs a bath when it gets home.

Meanwhile various thoughts come to mind. There will be authentic leadings of the Holy Spirit accompanied by plenty of our own ideas, good, bad or indifferent. There will be moments of confusion, occasions when we have to cope with gross temptations and times when we encounter Satan in the guise of an angel of light. However, sooner or later, we will find ourselves immersed in the place of stillness and peace, where God is to be found, and where the library of self-knowledge becomes the place where we can learn all kinds of truths about ourselves.

Transformation

If we keep the door of the heart tightly shut while at prayer, we won't easily connect with our deeper feelings and emotions. If we don't love ourselves with our own natural love, enriched by the love of God, we will find it hard to love God wholeheartedly and even though we perform many good deeds, we won't find it easy to love our neighbour as our own flesh.

Once we have ordered our lives and are faithfully keeping set times of prayer, we will begin to see the fruit in our daily lives. As prayer begins to overflow, we will reach the point where we are mindful of God's presence, even when we are fully occupied in seconding his proposals.

We will begin to see for ourselves that nothing, but nothing, "can separate us from the love of God which is in Christ Jesus."[10] As we abide in his love, the Holy Spirit enriches and transforms our natural love, so that we might better love ourselves as we gaze at our pale reflection in the mirror, first thing in the morning.

Unceasing prayer

Brother Lawrence,[11] formerly a soldier, footman and a hermit, wrote a little book called *The Practice of the Presence of God*. The title gives us a clue to the kind of life he lived. When he left the chapel to work in the monastery kitchen, his prayer continued. When it was suggested that it might be good if he spent an extra hour in chapel, he replied that he would be happy to do so, but tactfully suggested that it wouldn't add much to his continuing practice of unceasing prayer, while he worked contentedly in the kitchen amongst the pots and pans!

When Jane Chantal[12] kept set times of prayer in the chapel of the chateau, it is said that she was continually sending her servants on errands and was difficult and demanding. When her set times of prayer were complemented by the practice of ceaseless prayer, the prayer of loving attention, she was said to be quite different. Her staff no longer found her a burden but a blessing. In the solitude and silence of the oratory of the heart, the conflict between set times of prayer and the rigours of daily life ceased. Her prayer and active life were bound together with the golden thread of continuing prayer, so that others were blessed by her deepening spirituality. She had become a praying presence in the chateau.

It is, however, important to recognise that there is more to prayer than simply enjoying solitude and silence. Teresa of Avila[13] said, "I left for solitude, and very soon found that I was at war with myself."

The Helper

There are times when we wonder how we can be a praying presence in the world. How is it possible to be prayerful in a household of screaming children, when the only refuge is the bathroom? How do we begin to pray amidst the pressures of work or when a pneumatic drill is digging up the road? How can anyone begin to pray when they are seriously ill, devastated by bereavement or afflicted with any one of the severe trials of Job?

Further difficulties are faced by those called to withdraw to solitude and silence. They have to cope with loneliness by being lonely, boredom by feeling bored and restlessness by staying put. In addition to day-to-day frustrations, they have to deal with the emptiness which many in the world mask with activity.

To assist us in our labours Jesus left the promised gift of the Holy Spirit.[14] The Pentecostal movement continues to be a potent force in a sleepy Church, which is apt to forget that the Holy Spirit blows where it wills. At the feast of Pentecost the Holy Spirit fell upon the people out of the blue and took them by surprise.[15] As we continue to study the Scriptures, we see that the Holy Spirit was bestowed through baptism and the laying on of hands and prayer.[16] Look further and we come across the Holy Spirit descending upon Christian people all over again, as it did at the beginning.[17] In other words, although we ask for the Holy Spirit, he will come to our assistance at the time of his choosing. John Wesley had been praying that his heart would be warmed for a number of years before his well-documented spiritual awakening.

Jesus Christ encouraged his hearers to ask for the gift of the Holy Spirit for he said, "How much more shall your Father give the Holy Spirit to them that ask him?"[18]

The Gifts

When I was installed as a priest, I had to make a challenging response to what was required of me:

"I will, the Lord being my helper."

The gifts of the Holy Spirit[19] help us to discern and second God's proposals. They include wisdom and knowledge, which illuminate the soul and the mind, whereas faith strengthens the human will. Healing is a gift for service, while miracles declare the glory of God. Prophecy speaks God's word to God's people and discernment of spirits helps us to see what's what. The gift of tongues is the work of the Holy Spirit groaning within. It might be followed by praise, interpretation, prophecy or words of knowledge. St Paul's list of charisms is not exclusive and it is important to remember that they are gifts which might be given or withdrawn at any time. They come and go according to God's good pleasure. Going about God's business with the aid of the Holy Spirit is responding to our call to serve.

Fasting

Fasting, when I was a young man, included eating fish rather than meat on Fridays. Soon after the war, I was dining on a Friday with a devout Roman Catholic who ordered lobster (then an expensive luxury) and I well remember the look of surprise on my mother's face at what she considered to be empty legalism. The strict rules on fasting have long since been relaxed but responsible fasting continues to be an indispensable aid to prayer and is commended in the Gospel.

We don't abstain from food or drink so that we will appear on TV in the "weight watchers of the year" competition, but as a token of submission to God. We fast to bring the false self to heel and to let the true self off the hook. It is a little sacrifice in which we do our best to be conformed to the loving purposes of God, as we follow in the footsteps of our Lord Jesus Christ.

Fasting isn't hatred of the body; it isn't even total abstinence, but part of a spiritual training programme. We fast so that our energies might be aligned with the loving purposes of God. It is worthless if we stomp around like a bear with a sore head. Far better to be like the legendary St Rose,[20] who was so fearful that her complexion would betray her secret fasts, that she prayed that she would look radiant and lovely rather than pale and miserable. Fasting is one component in our preparation for the moment when we are called to let go of life itself, and return in humility to the outstretched arms of the Father.

Almsgiving

Almsgiving releases us from the entanglements of the false self by relinquishing our hold upon possessions. It isn't an occasional burst of generosity, but the recognition that all that we possess and all that we are is held in trust for God. Until this is imprinted upon our souls, we grudgingly part with a morsel of our meagre resources, slam down the lid of our treasure chest and sit tight.

Almsgiving is letting go. This doesn't mean that we are called to give everything away, fail to make provision for our own needs and beg on the streets, but to loosen our grip on all our dependences whether they be on a crust of bread, our homes, families, gifts or talents. We might not be called to embrace the poverty of St Francis of Assissi, but we are called to be poor in spirit.

Poverty of spirit is holding nothing back. Becoming our true selves involves cutting our ties with everything which prevents us from moving on with God. This doesn't mean that we avoid all social contact, give up valuable friendships, ignore family responsibilities, only take a bath once a year if we need it or not, refuse to have a meal out or take a taxi, but that we take care not to allow ourselves to be deterred by anyone, or anything, from seconding God's proposals.

Vocation

When I was twenty, I had been bogged down for three years in work which I didn't like; neither did I care much for what I saw in the mirror in the morning. I was mired in a quagmire of uncertainty. On the few occasions I had bared my soul and told others of my quest for meaning and purpose, no one seemed to understand my dilemma. I had a good job and good prospects, and my friends wondered why I complained. Outwardly all was well: inwardly I didn't know where I was going.

Then early one evening in November 1960, fifty years before this book was written, I received a telephone call. There was a lot of noise in the vestibule of the central YMCA and I struggled to hear, but the distinctive voice of a priest I knew asked, "David, when are you going to be a priest?"

I was overwhelmed. Only three years earlier I had decided that to offer myself for ordination was the last thing I wanted to do, but as soon as the question was asked, I knew that I would say yes.

In order to find a little space, I left the crowded and noisy vestibule and climbed the cold stone stairs to the chapel on the first floor. As I knelt in the pew at the front of the chapel, I was shaken by what I later learned to be a classic Pentecostal experience, an outpouring of the Holy Spirit, accompanied by speaking in tongues. The pilot light had done its work. My spirit came to life with a whoosh. I was overcome with joy. I was also embarrassed. I nervously looked around the chapel and was glad to see that I was alone.

At the time I had no idea what was happening, but I sensed that God loved me and that my vocation was to love him, to love myself and to love others, with a love enhanced by his love. Forty minutes later, dazed and shaken, I walked light-headedly down the grey stone stairs and came back down to earth.

Within days I had left my job at the Midland Bank. Almost two decades were to pass by before I began to understand what had happened. This was a personal Pentecost, which in my case came after both my baptism and confirmation and was unaccompanied by the laying on of hands and prayer. This anointing of the Holy Spirit strengthened me and enabled me to offer myself for training as a priest.

My mind cleared. My soul was bathed in love, joy and peace because I had been given a glimpse of what it is to be loved by God and I realised that it was time to stop running away from my vocation.

Each of us is called to be a praying presence and an enduring witness to the love of God, whether we are called to conduct great missionary campaigns or to stay quietly at home and do little things with great love. Being faithful to our own particular calling, by seconding each of God's proposals, is the beginning of a very long journey towards the goal of loving ourselves for the sake of God.

Notes

1. Luke 18.16.
2. St Bernard of Clairvaux. 1090–1153. *On loving God.* Caldey Isle Books. 1909. Argued that God should be loved because he is God!
3. I John 4.16.
4. Ephesians 5.29.
5. Mrs Alexander's well-known hymn No. 587. English Hymnal.
6. Friedrich Schleiermacher 1768–1834. Wrote 'Die Reden' for the cultured despisers of religion. He contended that religion was based on intuition and feeling (Anschauung und gefühl). A later work summing up his theology was based on the centrality of a feeling of 'absolute dependence upon God'.
7. John 4.14.
8. *Spiritual letters of Father Benson.* A. R. Mowbray & Co. Ltd. London and Oxford. 1924. p. 131.
9. Matthew 10.38–39.
10. Romans 8.39.
11. Brother Lawrence (Nicholas Herman 1605–1691). He worked and prayed in the monastery kitchen.
12. Saint Chantal 1572–1641. E. K. Sanders. SPCK. 1928. Together with Francis de Sales she formed the community known as the Visitation in 1610. It catered for those who couldn't cope with the more austere life of existing religious orders.
13. Teresa of Avila 1515–1582. See Chapter One note 9.
14. John 20.22.
15. Acts 2.1–12.
16. Acts 19.6.
17. Acts 10.44.
18. Luke 11.13.
19. I Corinthians 12.4–11.
20. St Rose of Lima 1586–1617. Renowned for her austerities. I read this anecdote in a children's book called *Six o'clock Saints* when I was a child. Other writings suggest that she deliberately spoiled her looks so that she wouldn't be married off!

Chapter Five

Wait for the Lord

Taizé

I was on sabbatical leave as I stood in a wayside garage not far from Bourges, wondering how to say 'automatic transmission' in French. Two hours later a skilled mechanic had crafted a new metal part on his lathe, repaired my car and charged me just nine francs. I had been travelling in my ten year old Humber Sceptre and as it spluttered along, with a leaky radiator, I had realised that my ailing vehicle reflected my own exhaustion.

It was a book on the subject of Christian unity, *Unité espérance de la vie,* by the prior Roger Schütz which had drawn my attention to the Taizé community and I was nearly there.

When I arrived, I slipped into the chapel where I slumped down on the floor, exhausted. In no time at all I found myself in floods of tears. It was as if a tap had been turned on. They seemed to be what the Eastern Church calls spiritual tears – not emotional, sad or bitter, but deeply refreshing – tears of sorrow mingled with joy.

I returned home armed with Taizé songs. One in particular has been a continuing source of strength and inspiration:

> Wait for the Lord, his day is near.
> Wait for the Lord, be strong take heart.[1]

Saint Benedict

Late in the fifth century, Benedict left the comforts of home and family to find space and time to wait upon the Lord. He spent three years in a cave at Subiaco. Triumphing over trials and tribulations, he was guided by the Holy Spirit, the helmsman in the voyage of love. Benedict was just nineteen years old when he left home and must have been sorely tempted to quit, to pursue a brilliant career and to hold a high position in society. He must have been tempted to abandon his vocation when monks, jealous of his spiritual gifts, attempted to poison him. Faithfully he stayed. What he learned in this challenging school of the Lord's service[2] helped him to shape a remarkable rule.

Originally prepared for lay monks, the Rule of St Benedict is a source of inspiration for all who endeavour to live balanced spiritual lives. One of the aims of the Rule was to help the monk to settle down, so it is not surprising that he was required to make a life-long vow of stability, a promise:

> to stay in one place
> to be loyal to his own community
> to be loyal to the abbot.

In other words, he was to abandon the fun and games of the gyrovague (i.e. someone who chases around looking for spiritual sensations and amazing preachers and who is always scurrying from one spiritual jamboree to another). At a time when bands of monks wandered around in droves and weren't always good news, Benedict's followers were required to forgo the practices of spiritual sensation seekers. The vow of stability was designed to discourage the fickle and unstable from joining the community. Benedict wanted to ensure that those who joined him in his venture were reliable.

The secret place

Christian prayer is an expression of a desire and willingness to play our own small part in building the Church upon the stable rock, which is Christ, rather than upon the shifting sands of enticing spiritual adventures. To build our spiritual home upon solid foundations is to be willing to put our whole self, body, mind and spirit, at God's disposal.

The call to prayer might never be a vocation to be a Trappist,[3] but to be a praying presence, whatever we are doing and wherever we are, be it going to the office as usual on Monday morning or staying at home with the children. Secular life isn't a barrier to prayer. Jesus never said that the only place to pray was in a church or a monastery. He taught us to find our own special place for prayer, a sanctuary, a secret place[4] in which to build an oratory in the heart. This might be anywhere suitably secluded – a quiet corner, a garden shed, the bathroom, or a long walk.

When a friend was considering fleeing to a monastery because he thought prayer would be less complicated there, Father Benson[5] reminded him of a saying of Thomas à Kempis: "If we put away one cross we will soon find another, and perhaps a heavier." And he added that it is not the world from which we escape, but the prince of this world, who can turn up anywhere.

Running away

Today people don't normally run away to the desert looking for spiritual thrills, but a cursory glance at the Sunday newspapers gives the game away. Our corporate mindset is as restless as a gyrovague. Travel advertisements focus on alluring dreams. If only you go to the Canary Islands life will be all sun, sea and intoxication. If you fly to the Caribbean you will meet the girl of your dreams emerging from the billowy brine. If you book this educational cruise you will find your soulmate. The restless urge to live our dream anywhere except where we are is unrewarding. It feeds on the unhelpful assumption that life in all its fullness can only be found somewhere else.

The heron

It was eleven o'clock in the evening. The street outside Church House, Westminster, was deserted. I was standing on the steps with John Pringle, founder of the NSF,[6] who was struggling with emphysema. I began to scuttle around looking for a taxi. It was already late and the streets of London were hushed. There wasn't a black cab in sight. Meanwhile, John Pringle studied me with a wry smile and said, "David, I'm a Scotsman and I have observed the heron. He stands on one leg and waits for the fish come to him."

I stopped fretting and stood silently beside him on the steps of Church House. Ten minutes later a black cab pulled up. God spoke to me through both the parable of the heron and an event; a word of wisdom and the arrival of a taxi. It was time to still the mind, rather than running around the corner and looking for a cab which wasn't there.

Stability isn't inertia. Stability is being content to be in the place where God has called us to be and to do what he requires. This doesn't mean that we can't lead active and creative lives, or go away on a well-deserved holiday for a rest and a change; but we mustn't allow feelings, emotions, wants or desires to blow us off course.

Beneath an outward show of conformity, the human soul is often like an untrained filly who would rather do her own thing, whether it be to stand on her hind legs and kick when required to be still, or to lie indolently in the warm straw in the corner of the steamy stable when it's time to go into the yard to exercise.

How often do we glibly say, "I will do anything for you Lord," and then fail to notice that we have done the opposite. How happily we praise the Lord on Palm Sunday but where are we on Good Friday? We go to our prayers and ask God to teach us to "seek for no reward save knowing that we do thy will."[7] And then we go our own way.

The untamed filly is that part of our fallen human nature which has been deceived by the cunning of the prince of this world into believing that it is all right to do anything we choose – that it is all right to do what we want, when we want, without any reference to God or to the needs of others.

Staying put

John Pringle's words addressed my instability. As I ponder that moment over thirty years ago, I recall the teaching of the epistle of St James concerning the importance of not trying to force the pace, but going with the flow of God's will.[8] Our Christian reward isn't to be found amongst the world's glittering prizes but by staying put in our appointed place, equally willing to engage in active service or to sit in silence at the feet of Jesus. Stability is being where God has called us to be. Unless and until he calls us to move, this is where we are required to stay.

It's foolish to fritter our lives away thinking we would rather be round the next corner, or to go to work saying to ourselves, "I don't want to be doing this boring job for the rest of my life." Our vocation is to second God's proposals. Where we are is where God has called us to stay put as a praying presence, until the very moment the removal van pulls up at the front door.

A still mind

When our minds are buzzing with unnecessary and irrelevant information which hinders prayer, we don't have to clear up on our own. We immerse ourselves in the ocean of God's love and surf the vibrant waves of his mercy as they roll up the beach, clearing away the junk and debris. In their wake, they leave the magical beauty of the clear golden sands and deposit seeds of new life. What comes in on the surge is true, honourable, lovely and of good report.

Stilling the mind in prayer is like preparing for a long journey so that we know where we are going. As we study the map, we focus on our destination and purpose. We make a note of the main roads and significant landmarks, while ensuring that we don't become overladen with extraneous detail. If we focus on what is important, we are less likely to get lost.

Silence and acceptance

In the secret place we find solitude for prayer. Unused to silence or being alone, we might well feel anxious and confused. The remedy is not to try to escape by finding things to occupy the mind, but to accept that we withdraw to do a detox from overactivity.

In the oratory of the heart we learn to glorify God by existing. We pray that we may have the wisdom and humility to accept the things we cannot change. We come to terms with the fact that we are called to take no thought for the morrow and that we cannot add a cubit to our stature by thought.

To live by faith is to be positive. The faith by which we live is not faith in ourselves but in God. Positive thinking is at best a half truth. It is naïve to believe that anyone can be Pope or win an Olympic gold medal. Although God provides, his provision might be just enough to sustain a church mouse rather than to help the rich young man to heap up more riches. To live by faith is to be willing to pass through the eye of a needle, while continuing on the straight and narrow way which leads to glory. Those who have stable hearts and minds don't put God to the test; they gladly place their trust in Our Lord, who has promised to be with us now and until the end of time.[9]

Self-forgetfulness

My grandmother went to a finishing school in Paris in the 1890s. There she was taught that a lady looking in the mirror, while preparing herself to face the world, should pay careful attention to her dress and make-up. As soon as this was done, she was urged to forget about the way she looked, and to go out with assurance and aplomb.

As we forget about ourselves and focus on Christ, we gradually become less preoccupied with our own interests and discover deep and tender shoots of neighbourly love. We see the person we pass on the street in a new way. We are drawn to the presence of Christ in them. We see the love of Christ enfold them. As we behold the presence of the living Christ in the world, we are less inclined to avert our eyes from sadness and pain. We see the beauty of God in the lonely and the unloved. We see the beauty of Christ in those who know not, or care not, for our Lord and Saviour Jesus Christ. We see the beauty of Christ in unexpected places.

In prayer we become more alive to spiritual reality. We rejoice with those who rejoice and weep with those who weep. We also see the ravages of sin.

An unstable mind is self-obsessed. It is preoccupied with its own wants and selfish interests. It runs around looking for more and more excitements, which are like the addictive Turkish Delight, given to the child Edmund in the story by C. S. Lewis. The more he ate, the more he craved. The more he craved, the more he ate. The more he ate, the more sick he became.

An unstable and divided mind is as fickle as the restless Athenian who couldn't hear the Gospel message because he always wanted to hear some new thing.[10]

Posture

Stability is also a requirement for the body. Prayer is never easy if we are preoccupied with bodily discomfort, so it is advisable to try to find a position in which we are relaxed. A good posture helps us to still ourselves for prayer. My favoured position is that adopted by Richard Rolle[11] who wrote:

> "I have loved to sit for no penance, nor fantasy nor that I wished men to talk of me, not for no such thing: but only because I knew that I loved God more, and longer lasted in the comfort of love than going, or standing, or kneeling. For sitting I am most at rest, and my heart most upward. But therefore peradventure it is not best that another should sit, as I did and will do to my death, save he were disposed in soul as I was."

A stable intent

Prayer is built on a stable intent, that is a continuing disposition of goodwill towards God and men, which underlies all we think, say or do.

A good intent is a deep-rooted desire to be united with God both in love and in purpose. A good intent is receptive to the Gospel and centres the heart on God. A good intent is the cement which holds prayer, work and life together. Whether we are aware of it or not, such a state of goodwill underpins the life of prayer. Waking or sleeping, it is there. When we are preoccupied with matters which require our wholehearted attention it is there. A good intent is the breeding ground for ceaseless prayer and gives rise to peace and harmony in the soul.

When the body, mind and spirit are settled, we are better able to hear God's communications. Maybe this is why God often chooses to speak to us in the silent hours of the night.

Not racing ahead

Not long ago I dreamt that a railway train, painted bright Buckingham green, was speeding down the line through lush green pastures. It was clattering along at a reckless speed, so I was not a little alarmed when I saw that I was the driver. I was donned in an old-fashioned railwayman's uniform. I could see that the train was going far too quickly and was heading for a crash.

As I reflected upon the dream, I realised that in my waking life I had been too busy to notice warning signs telling me to slow down. While asleep, I could hear what God was saying. The dream seemed to be telling me not to race on ahead of God's proposals in a particular matter. It gave me an opportunity to avoid a crisis by putting on the brakes. Even if my heart was in the right place, I was still running on ahead of instructions!

Bishop John Hare, who was the Bishop of Bedford in the 1970s, wrote an article in the Diocesan newspaper after he had suffered a heart attack. He had been going about his Diocesan duties when he collapsed. As he came round, he asked his driver where he was. The reply: "In Luton." The Bishop exclaimed, "I can't die in Luton." He climbed back into the car and was driven home. The lesson to be learned, he wrote, is that our bodies speak to us. We must listen. God had been speaking to him through his body for some time and he hadn't been listening. It was telling him not to overdo it.

A verse from a psalm cautions us not to run on ahead of God's proposals:

> "If the Lord does not build the house, then is their labour lost who build it."[12]

Stability is the way of peace. This is not the peace of a long summer holiday, lying on sun-drenched beaches in the Caribbean. Neither is it the peace of those who are complacent, cut off or repressed. It is the peace of God which isn't dependent upon outward circumstances or surface feelings. It is a deep peace. It is the peace of God which passes all understanding. It is the peace of a clear conscience.

Obedience

Obedience is a sensitive subject in the climate of today. It is sometimes mistakenly considered to be the enemy of creativity. Maybe we shouldn't be surprised that after the legacy of the Victorian age, and even more the cruel dictatorships of the twentieth century, people fear the autocratic.

But Christian obedience isn't servility. To be obedient is to hear. Catechesis is trying to make people hear.

The Benedictine abbot isn't a dictator. He is elected by the monks who place their trust in his wisdom. The abbot is a *servus servorum dei*, a servant of the servants of God.

The vow of stability provides a safe environment for the monk to focus on the *opus Dei*, the work of God. The stable monk also puts the interests of the community above his own wants and desires. In the world we have comparable duties and responsibilities. There are those we are called to obey and those we are called to serve. We obey those whom we are called to obey unless our conscience sounds the alarm.

When I was a curate, the rector rang me at 2 a.m. and asked me to feed his horses in a field close by. I might have said that feeding his horses was not a part of my job description. In the event, I struggled out of bed and was richly rewarded, because on a moonlit night the horses were delighted to see me, laden with their bales of straw.

However, the duty of obedience can never be wheeled out as an excuse for ignoring our consciences or defending what is wrong! A well-informed conscience is to be obeyed. When invited to drink a toast to the Pope, Cardinal John Henry Newman, a loyal Roman Catholic, said that first he would drink a toast to conscience and only then would he drink a toast to the Pope.

The blank mind

In the secret place of prayer we enter solitude and silence. In stillness we empty our minds of everything, so that we may come to a deeper awareness of God and be open to fresh insights about ourselves.

A man I knew went to see a psychotherapist. After a ten-minute silence the client was asked what he was thinking. He replied, "Nothing. My mind is blank." From time to time the question and answer were repeated: "What are you thinking about?" "My mind is a blank." This continued for an hour. At the second session the same thing happened again. After the third session the client decided not to return. He told me that he felt unhappy about having to write a cheque for another session of what he considered to be a waste of time and money. The therapist had failed to lure the tortoise from his shell. The silence wasn't the peace of God but a lockout from the soul.

Rather than cutting us off from ourselves, authentic prayer is the key which gives us access to the deeper places of the heart. If our minds are lazy, inactive, cut off or repressed, the Holy Spirit helps us to

> wake up
> face up to things
> not leave things undone
> learn to say yes
> think more about others
> think more about God.

The overactive mind

If our minds are manic and overactive and allow a continuing stream of irrelevant information, wandering thoughts and temptations to buzz around unchallenged, the Holy Spirit will assist us in the work of renewal by helping us to

> consciously put on the brakes
> clear out the rubbish
> focus on the present moment
> not dwell on the past or worry about the future
> trust God at all times.

A stable mind guides us along the middle way between saying, "God calling" every time the phone rings and allowing ourselves to be at the mercy of everything that wantonly invades our privacy.

Our personal Subiaco

Jesus Christ was the model of stability. He never strayed from the place where he was called to be. In his childhood years he stayed at home and honoured his father and mother. He didn't hesitate to be about his Father's business when he visited the temple at the age of only twelve.[13] He stayed in the building trade for a number of years, glorifying God by his loving obedience and the creative work of his own hands.

He was faithful in the three years of his active ministry, in which he demonstrated by his life and example what it means to love God and to love our neighbour.

In Holy Week he didn't waver but stayed put in Jerusalem. On Maundy Thursday, he walked across the Kedron valley to the Mount of Olives to pray and to wait. He didn't desert his post in the Garden of Gethsemane. He didn't run away from the ascent to Calvary and throughout, he was faithful in prayer. His final words, the words used by every Jewish child before he falls asleep, were simple words of trust: "Father into thy hands I commend my spirit."[14]

The keys to stability and peace are to be found in the wise words I first sang in the community chapel at Taizé in a moment of spiritual renewal:

> Wait for the Lord, his day is near.
> Wait for the Lord, be strong take heart.[15]

Notes

1. Words from the Taizé songbook based on Psalm 27.14. The Taizé community in Burgundy was constituted in 1949. It developed under the leadership of Roger Schütz and attracted the young from far and wide. A council for youth was launched in the 1970s.
2. The school of the Lord's service. The Rule originally prepared by Benedict was for laymen rather than priests and was noted for its leniency.
3. Trappists. Popular name of reformed Cistercians. The reform began in La Trappe in 1664 and continues to this day.
4. Matthew 6.6.
5. *Spiritual letters of Father Benson*. A.R. Mowbray and Co. Ltd. London and Oxford. 1924. p. 152.
6. The National Schizophrenia Fellowship. Today known as Rethink.
7. Words of the prayer of St Ignatius beginning, "Teach us good Lord."
8. James 4.15.
9. Matthew 28.20.
10. Acts 17.21.
11. Richard Rolle. Taken from Thomas Merton. *Spiritual Direction, Meditation and What is Contemplation?* Anthony Clarke. Wheathampstead. 1975. p. 68.
12. Psalm 127.1.
13. Luke 2.48–50.
14. Luke 23.46.
15. See Note 1 above.

Chapter Six

Five a day

Contemplation, meditation and vocal prayer

We are unlikely to be able to identify or acknowledge the contemplative dimension of prayer, unless we are in a position to compare it with the meditative and vocal. A contemplative disposition is to be observed in the wondering gaze of a small child. It is a primitive part of our God-given make-up, which we cannot begin to understand until we reach maturity. Wonder, love and praise are as much the province of the small child as the advanced contemplative. The babe in his mother's arms is a natural contemplative when he beholds his mother's face. He is meditative when he can identify the face of his mother and lovingly stretches out a hand to gently touch it. His praise and joy know no bounds when expressed vocally, as he first begins to speak.

Beginners

When we begin to pray, we use vocal prayers and spiritual reading. Vocal prayer includes set prayers said silently or aloud, together with psalms, hymns and spiritual songs. We use our own spoken prayers and, from time to time, sharp-shooting targeted prayers called arrow prayers. We also participate in the vocal prayer in church services.

From the outset of the way of prayer, it is not unusual to be aware of a sense of love, joy and peace. Warm spiritual feelings, sometimes referred to as consolations,[1] aren't easy to describe. They are moments of intense joy and delight when we are very blessed and they might feel very rewarding. However, they are not the substance of prayer but spoonfuls of sugar to make the medicine go down. Consolations aren't the meat of prayer but encouraging treats for beginners.

If we pine for consolations and spiritual experiences without attempting to live the Gospel life, we will lose sight of our ultimate goal, which is to be at one with God both in love and in purpose. If we cling to consolations and depend upon them, then when they evaporate, we will be tempted to abandon prayer.

Preparation

Preparation for prayer is more than taking a few deep breaths. It includes the enrichment of the whole of our lives by the care we take in the way we live. The more attentive we are to God during the day, the better equipped we will be in our set times of prayer. The more disciplined we are in keeping set times of prayer, the more open and responsive we will be to God during the day.

The three different modes of prayer,

> contemplation
> meditation
> vocal prayer

are different modes of one reality. They are three parts of a single whole. The three parts form a kind of trinity. Although distinct, they are interconnected. It isn't always easy to see where one ends and the other begins and any or each of these modes of prayer might occur at any time – sometimes at the same time.

Contemplation

Contemplation, about which I will say more in subsequent chapters, is paying loving attention to God. Contemplation is an underlying state of receptiveness to the presence of God. Contemplation is the adoration of God in the deep recesses of the human heart, with or without the accompaniment of words and images. Contemplation issues in an eruption of love and praise, as we behold the presence and creative activity of God, constantly renewing the cosmos and infusing life into the soul.

Meditation

Thomas Merton wrote,

> "Meditation is really very simple and there is not much need for elaborate techniques to teach us how to go about it. But that does not mean that mental prayer can be practised without constant and strict interior discipline. This is especially true in our own time, when the intellectual and moral flabbiness of a materialistic society has robbed man's nature of its spiritual energy and tone – there is a difference between being strict and being rigid – the well-disciplined soul is supple and adaptable."[2]

Meditation is stocking the cellars of the soul with spiritual treasures through looking, pondering and reflecting. It is the work of the imagination and intellect.

One way to meditate is by using the visual imagination to stir the heart. This warm Franciscan method employs imaginative immersion in the Gospel followed by spiritual reflection. "We see this thing which is come to pass and the babe lying in a manger."[3] We do not think about the virtue of humility, nor do we ponder the divinity of the man born to be King. Our creative imagination conveys us to the stable, so that we may kneel beside the shepherds and adore the infant Christ. In our mind's eye we are there. In this way, we walk with Jesus all the way from the stable to the Easter Garden.

Another method of meditation engages both the imagination and the intellect. For example we choose a scene from the Gospel, picture it, think about it and learn lessons about how to live. St Ignatius of Loyola,[4] a former soldier and founder of the Jesuits, developed an advanced version of such a scheme. The bare bones are as follows:

> We tidy up our hearts and minds, deal with sin, and try to eliminate self-will.
> We still our minds and focus on the presence of God.
> We choose a subject for meditation (e.g. from the Gospel).
> We use our imagination to set the scene and cogitate before extracting whatever lesson is appropriate for the day.
> We make a positive resolution.

Although this seems to be like praying by numbers, all may benefit from the employment in prayer of the memory (as we recall or visualise a subject), the mind or imagination (as we ponder what we see) and the will (as we resolve to enrich our lives by living what we have learned).

St Francis de Sales[5] suggested using the imagination to place ourselves in the presence of God, by

> taking delight that God is everywhere
> pondering Jesus our Saviour
> picturing him
> looking within our hearts and rejoicing that God is present.

Once we are settled in the secret place, we ask God to help us through the coming day. We ponder our chosen portion of the Gospel and express our love for God. We consider how the passage we have used might best shape our life. For example we might decide to be more loving, forgiving, generous etc. The meditation ends with thanksgiving.

A well-known pattern of meditation, devised for the formation of priests, was developed by L. Tronson, the Superior General of St. Sulpice,[6] in the late seventeenth century. It looks complicated but is easily summarised. In this method there are three significant steps:

Jesus in the eyes
Jesus in the heart
Jesus in the hands.

Jesus in the eyes is Jesus in our spiritual seeing. As we meditate, we use either the imagination or the intellect to visualise or reflect upon any aspect of the Gospel, or we may ponder the living presence of the risen Christ. Once again the creative imagination is brought into play. What we see, what we feel, what we think and what we learn, fortifies the will and kindles the flame of love in the soul. Our purpose is to open the eye of the soul (Jesus in the eyes), warm the heart (Jesus in the heart), and fill the cellars of the soul with good things so that we may better serve God and our fellow men (Jesus in the hands).

Having given the barest outline of typical patterns of meditation, I have to own that I have been incapable of following any one of these practices on a regular basis. Nevertheless, I often find myself employing either the intellect or the creative imagination while reading, preparing a sermon or walking to the post, as I ponder the things of God. Each of us has to find our own way to stock the cellars of the soul. The best paintings aren't done by numbers.

Prayer is multi-layered so that while saying a set prayer, such as the Lord's Prayer, we might be reflecting upon the meaning of the words as we say them, or we might be gently lifted up into contemplative prayer as words lose their significance, while the soul is gently suspended in the love of God.

Vocal prayer

Vocal prayer is stoked by the following **five a day**. Firstly comes:

Adoration and praise

Prayers of praise build on the opening words of the Lord's Prayer, "Hallowed be thy name." Praise is the summit of prayer. Praise is the heart of all worship. Praise is ascribing value. Praise is obedience to the first great commandment. Praise declares who it is we worship. Praise lifts us up out of ourselves, detaches us from our own concerns and sets us free to love and adore.

It has been said that when the three wise men came to the stable, they weren't concerned about themselves, so they didn't make long speeches but knelt in silence and humility beside the man born to be king. Praise is an overflowing of godly love which brings joy to the whole man, body, mind and spirit. Praise is drinking freely from the river of life. Praise is the outpouring of unaffected joy.

The discipline of praising God is the most effective way of ensuring that our hearts are in the right place, as we focus our attention on the one who alone is good, but the time will come when words fail and we simply lift up our hearts.

Praise and adoration are also expressed in word, song or dance, either in the secret place or in public worship. Praise can be released in an outpouring of singing in tongues.

Praise is an expression of humility which sets us free from the clutches of deep-rooted self-centredness. The first of the great commandments isn't that we should think about the Lord our God, but that we should love him. Praise, whether offered from a sense of duty, through gritted teeth or from a loving heart, opens the door to God's transforming love, so that we show forth his praise not only with our lips but in our lives.

Praise and adoration are complemented by:

Thanksgiving

Because God has our deepest interests at heart, we offer prayers of thanksgiving. Sometimes they are spontaneous. Sometimes we feel as bogged down as a child writing thank you letters to distant uncles and aunts on Boxing Day.

There is so much to thank God for. When God saw all that he had made, he saw that it was very good. Even in our trials and sufferings we thank God, because "he works all things together for good for those who love him."[7] We don't thank God for our misfortunes, but we may thank him in them. We continue to thank God for his goodness whatever our circumstances.

Every day we thank God for all good things. We thank God for our homes, our families, our friends, our life, our health, our food and all good things both spiritual and natural.

The corporate act of thanksgiving is the Anamnesis, the representation of the Last Supper, called the Eucharist. The word Eucharist means thanksgiving. In this service we offer ourselves, our souls and bodies, while our Lord offers us divine life. During the Eucharist we taste and see that the Lord is good.

In the Eucharist we recall the great mystery that on the same night that he was betrayed, Jesus offered himself up, as he took bread in his holy and blameless hands and gave thanks and praise.[8] Jesus gave his life so that we might live. The Eucharist is the supreme act of worship in which we rejoice that Christ, who is raised from the dead, is with us and in us.

Petition

Jesus said, "Ask and it shall be given unto you; seek and ye shall find."[9] He made it clear that we should make our requests known unto God. He also taught us to bless and curse not. Although we make petitions, we do our best to ask for what is good, either for ourselves or for others. From the events in the Garden of Gethsemane,[10] we learn that Jesus did not want to endure the pain and suffering of the Cross. This desire to avoid suffering was trumped by something he wanted even more – to do the will of the Father. As he wrestled in prayer, he sought the strength to do the Father's will.

When we pray, "Give us this day our daily bread," we are asking God to provide. But the Greek can also be construed as meaning that we are asking for tomorrow's bread today, that we are asking for the bread of God to help us to do the will of the one that he has sent. In other words, our daily bread includes bread from the bakery and bread from heaven. It also includes the material and spiritual resources we need, to enable us to be the person God wants us to be and to do what he wants us to do.

There is an important distinction between what we need and what we want. For this reason we know that when we make our requests known unto God he may say

> Yes – if we ask for what is good and of God.
> Wait – if it's not the right time.
> No – if the answer is "My grace is sufficient for you."

or he might be silent, because we are required to trust him. Silence invites us to continue to pray, "Thy will be done."

God, the judge of all that is good, gives good gifts to his children and we are assured of the promised gift of the Holy Spirit, which God will grant to all those who ask.[11]

Intercession

Intercession is praying for others. We come into the presence of God before we wade in with requests. We put our hopes and fears aside because we aren't alone. To intercede is to join the heavenly intercession of Christ. We try to fathom for whom and how he wants us to pray and then we pray as best we can. Our own preoccupations might point in one direction. The loving purposes of God might point in another. We cast our cares upon him and to prevent us from becoming overburdened with heaviness and sorrow, we accompany intercession with praise.

Confession

In preparing for confession we look honestly at ourselves, repent of wrongdoing, tackle false attitudes and note what we have left undone. We say sorry to God and ask his forgiveness. There is no point in saying sorry unless we mean it. It is better to wait until the sorrow is real. Public lamentation and breast beating without a genuine change of heart is not good enough. The prodigal repented long before he saw his father. The older brother never did. The evidence of sincere repentance is the willingness to own up, to put matters right, to humble ourselves and amend our lives.

This five a day is a balanced diet of vocal prayer. It is the leaven which raises us up to another level of living. Sometimes it's easy. At other times we experience barrenness, aridity, emptiness and a feeling that God's presence is hidden.

When we experience accidie, or feeling fed up with prayer, we first examine ourselves to see if the lights have gone out because of our carelessness or sin. If we find that there are no major obstacles of our own making, we accept that God might have hidden his presence to encourage us to move into the deeper waters of prayer. The point at which many come to a full stop is when they become disillusioned with prayer because it feels barren and empty. They think they have failed. But this is where prayer really begins. Many back off at this point but it is essential to hold on.

Spiritual reading

The Scriptures may be read like any other book. However, in prayer the Spirit might lead us from the Lectio (spiritual reading) which feeds the mind, to the Lectio which feeds the soul. This Lectio is the launchpad which enables the soul to take off, by enabling the words to convey us from literal meaning which feeds the mind, to spiritual engagement. The reading takes us beyond our human thoughts into the place of spiritual reality in which the whole man is touched – body, mind and spirit. For example the words, "I am the bread of life,"[12] awaken us to the real presence of the risen Christ in the present moment. We are conveyed beyond words to another realm. This is more than feeding the mind with active or reflective meditation; it is seeing with the eye of the soul. It is more than entering into a deeper understanding of the extraordinary generosity of Jesus Christ in giving his life; it is being lifted across the threshold into supra-conceptual spiritual reality. It is both insight and outsight. Such seeing is a gift. We can't make it happen any more than we can turn on the Northern Lights. But we can be in the right place so that we don't miss the display.

Aspirations

As we advance in the spiritual life and the storehouse of the soul is well stocked, prayer sometimes comes from nowhere. We wake up in the night saying the Lord's Prayer. By day we find that prayers simply escape. An account of this type of prayer is given by St Paul, who speaks about the Holy Spirit groaning within.[13] "Aspirations" is the word generally used for prayers which simply happen. They escape without our having made any conscious decision to pray.

Loving attention

Prayer takes us beyond words. The prayer of loving attention is like being in a room with someone very close. The silence isn't empty. It's a silence of trusting love. And yet we are hesitant to be with the one we love because we are anxious about neglecting the active and necessary work of Martha.[14] We don't find it easy to be like Mary, sitting at the feet of Jesus while saying and doing nothing. Our caution is understandable and it is good to take care that withdrawal into the secret place isn't an escape from responsibilities, but opening the door of the heart so that, filled with the Holy Spirit, we may better serve both God and man.

Doubts

Satan will skilfully play on our doubts and fears. He takes note if our thoughts stray back to the occupations and pleasures of the world. He knows that we are vulnerable when our props are removed. Questions will torment us. What could I be doing for my children and grandchildren? What could I be doing here in the village? What about the poor, the lonely and the unloved? What about the unconverted? Why am I in this lonely place sitting on my butt feeling gloomy, useless and disengaged, when there is so much to be done?

He tries to make us forget that God loves our families, our local community and those in spiritual need infinitely more than we do. He tries to make us forget that in the midst of our trials and tribulations, we can hold our heads up high because our salvation is nearer than when we first believed.[15] In a nutshell, he undermines our confidence by working on our fragility. Our vocation is to love – to love those whom God has called us to love, to love in his time and in his way. They may not be the ones at the top of our list but the ones at the top of his. They could even be our enemies![16]

Should we preen ourselves because we have committed our lives to prayer, the adversary will not be slow to sow seeds of complacency, which will beget weeds of self-righteousness. He will persuade us that a little folding of the hands, a little silence, a little rest, is the prayer. He will suggest that if we put a candle on the table, look into the flickering light, empty the mind, drift off into a cosy haze, maybe even with a glass of something at hand, we are half way to being a saint. After employing this "rope a dope" strategy, he carefully slips out of the room, having stolen our resolution to clear away all self-centred preoccupations so that we may be filled with the costly love of the Lamb that was slain.

Focus

Prayer is focussing on God with the eye of the soul. By focus, I don't have in mind a photographer running around trying to line up his camera before a moving object vanishes, but the gaze of a babe in his mother's arms. The babe expresses his love for his mother with a look of wondering love. He cannot make a long speech. He can't even speak. His unmitigated joy is expressed in long silences interspersed with a contented gurgle. The prelude to contemplative prayer is a look of wondering love.

At all times, we do our best to strike a balance between prayer and daily living, between focussing on God and being wholly engaged in what God requires of us, for it hardly needs to be said that it isn't possible or desirable to try to be saying vocal prayers all day. If we attempted to do this, we would soon be frazzled. In any case, it is important to remember that prayer is not tying ourselves up in knots by imposing an impossible burden on the mind; it is letting go and forgetting, while gently allowing streams of living water to flow into the soul. To be at prayer during the day is as gentle an activity as a dog lying on the mat, waiting for his master to come home. He isn't doing anything. He's quiet and still. But he's attentive and alert. He's always ready to jump up at any moment.

In set times of prayer, a fire is lit in the oratory of the heart. To pray without ceasing is to return, whenever necessary, to prod the fire with a poker, add more fuel or apply the bellows. We keep the fire alight with the recitation of a prayer, firing off an arrow prayer, contemplative prayer, or being actively engaged in seconding God's proposals. At times, we are simply called to sit by the fire and keep warm.

Whenever the fire of love dies down, we fan the flames to ensure that we continue to be a praying presence, wherever we are and whatever we are doing.

St Cuthbert

Should we begin to think that the weak effort of our heart is too demanding, a moment's reflection upon the commitment and practice of St Cuthbert[17] will soon sober us up. He didn't go to a cold church wrapped in a warm cloak at 7.30 a.m., to say Morning Prayer. He didn't go downstairs to a centrally heated kitchen in his dressing gown to make a hot mug of tea before sitting comfortably. He didn't even stay in his monk's cell, surrounded by books and his meagre belongings. St Cuthbert's praise, thanksgiving, intercessions, petitions and confessions were not infrequently offered in the ice-cold waters of the North Sea, where he stood wrapped in prayer for half the night!

Perhaps his example may encourage us to have a little more steel, to be a little more rigorous in our endeavours to join in and live the prayer of St Richard of Chichester[18] – that we might "see thee more clearly, love thee more dearly and follow thee more nearly day by day."

Notes

1. See Chapter Seven page 89. Spiritual feelings in this case are the sensory joys experienced by beginners in prayer.
2. Thomas Merton. *Spiritual Direction and Meditation and What is Contemplation.* Anthony Clarke. Wheathampstead. 1975. p. 63.
3. Luke 2.15.
4. Ignatius Loyola. Retired for a period of solitude and extreme mortification in Manresa. Prepared the Spiritual Exercises and was the founder of the Jesuits. He died in 1556.
5. Francis de Sales 1567–1622. Bishop of Geneva. Known for his remarkable gifts of spiritual direction. Under his wing, Jane Chantal built up the religious community known as the Visitation.
6. Saint Sulpice was a congregation of secular priests founded in Paris in 1642. L. Tronson, the superior general from 1676, developed the Sulpician method of prayer.
7. Romans 8.28.
8. I Corinthians 11.23–26.
9. Matthew 7.7.
10. Luke 22.42.
11. John 14.13ff.
12. John 6.48.
13. Romans 8.26.
14. Luke 10.38ff.
15. Romans 13.11.
16. Matthew 5.44.
17. St Cuthbert retired to the Farne Islands in 676 AD, where he remained as a hermit for eight years. He died in the year 687.
18. Richard became Bishop of Chichester in 1244.

Chapter Seven

The raising and beating of the wings

In a sermon preached just after the war, Bishop Leonard Wilson[1] who had suffered in Changi gaol said:

> "I remember Archbishop Temple in one of his books writing that if we pray for any particular virtue, whether it be patience, courage or love, one of the answers God gives to us is an opportunity for expressing that virtue. After my first beating I was almost afraid to pray for courage lest I should have another opportunity of exercising it, but my unspoken prayer was there, and without God's help I doubt whether I should have come through. Long hours of ignoble pain were a severe test. In the middle of that torture they asked me if I still believed in God. When by God's help I said 'I do' they asked me why God did not save me, and by the help of the Holy Spirit I said, 'God does save me. He does not save me by freeing me from pain and punishment, but he saves me by giving me the spirit to bear it.' And when they asked me why I did not curse them, I told them that it was because I was a follower of Jesus Christ.
>
> "By the grace of God I saw those men not as they were, but as they had been. Once, they were little children playing with their brothers and sisters and happy in their parents' love, in those far off days before they had been conditioned by their false nationalistic ideals – and it is hard to hate little children. But even that was

not enough. There came to my mind, as I lay on the table, the words of the communion hymn[2]:

> Look Father, look on his anointed face
> And only look on us as found in Him."

Just before the service in which I was to be ordained deacon in 1967, Bishop Leonard Wilson came into the vestry and stood quietly for a few moments before saying a short prayer. He was a praying presence. St Peter's Church was spiritually alive long before we began to process down the aisle singing, "Christ is made the sure foundation."

Cooperative contemplation

Love and mercy are essential components of prayer because

> God is love
> God loves us
> We are called to love God
> We are called to love one another.[3]

Contemplation is a cooperative venture. It is called infused because, although passive contemplation is a pure gift of God over which we have no say, the word contemplation itself suggests that contemplating is something we do.

St Francis de Sales illustrated the two-way process of active contemplative prayer by using the model of a bird, like a fulmar, which can hardly stand. Just as the bird can't take off until it raises its wings, so in order to lift up our hearts in prayer, we need to make a conscious decision. And just as a gust of wind lifts the bird off its feet, so the Holy Spirit raises us up. The raising and the beating of the wings in flight represent the cooperation of the soul with God.

Contemplation continues to be active so long as we are doing anything whatsoever to fuel the prayer. Going to the secret place, vocal prayers, meditations or movements of the heart are all active. So too is posture, or even silence, if accompanied by appropriate movements of the will.

Contemplative moments which come out of the blue are called passive. Such moments occur without any conscious decision or action on our part. St Isaac the Syrian[4] noted that such pure contemplative moments separate prayer from the lips.

Active contemplation

When I returned from my CACTM selection conference in Sheffield (following which I was recommended for training for the ordained ministry in the Church of England), I spent a few days on retreat in St Catherine's Stepney, where I was enfolded in silence. Words and symbols had little to say. I simply wanted to be with God. After two or three days of complete silence, it was time to catch the bus home. The disappointment that it was all over was like the way one feels at the end of an idyllic summer holiday, which one hoped would never end. Small talk, talk of any kind, broke the spell.

This experience of peace, however, wasn't the spiritual experience of the advanced contemplative which isn't easily disturbed, but the peace of the inexperienced beginner, which sustained me for a while, before passing by as quietly as a ship in the night. When I awoke in the morning and looked out to sea, the ship was gone.

The joys of making merry on the nursery slopes of prayer came to an end, as I encountered the first icy blasts of aridity and desolation. My eyes were opened and I began to see that to make any real progress in prayer, we must be prepared for the hard yards and be well equipped for a long climb.

Brother Albert

"Brother Albert lay dying. His countenance was aflame and shone with a celestial light, which rendered it so marvellously beautiful that all were enraptured, and silently shed tears of joy. Suddenly he cried out, 'Oh I have seen it, I have seen it, I have seen it!' and lowering his arms, he crossed them on his breast. St John of the Cross, who was present, hastened to ask Brother Albert, who was in a state of ecstasy, 'What have you seen, what have you seen?' And he answered, 'Love, love!'"[5]

The journey from the beginner's blessings to the dying raptures of the contemplative Brother Albert is the journey of a lifetime.

Words fail

One of the trials endured by those who have made a little progress in prayer is discovering that words which have been so full of meaning lose their power. Previously inspirational words become inadequate and meaningless.

The frustrations experienced when words become impotent are not unlike those experienced in a human love affair, such as that portrayed in the desperate words of Eliza Doolittle in the musical *My Fair Lady*, who cries out in exasperation, "Words, words, words! I'm so sick of words! Don't talk of love – show me!"

After they had walked the Emmaus road[6] and stopped at an inn, words failed the two disciples. It was only when their animated conversation came to an end, it was only when they paused for a rest, that they knew Jesus in the breaking of the bread. Filled with wonder and amazement, their eyes were opened as they beheld the risen Christ. Words didn't fail because they were defective, but because they had become unnecessary. When they saw the risen Christ, their hearts were strangely warmed. They looked at one another and said, "Did not our hearts burn within us while we were on the way?"

Passive prayer, in which we enter the joy of Christ, is pure gift. Silently and unexpectedly, our Lord takes us by the hand; he wordlessly speaks of love as he draws us into the stillness of his presence so that, like Mary at the feet of Jesus, we may worship and adore.

I am reminded of a day just after the war, when cars were rare and new cars unheard of. We were walking to school when a neighbour with a brand new sports car unexpectedly drew up and gave us a lift. Contemplation is passive when it is surprising, unexpected and a pure gift of God.

Affective prayer

Those who have made headway in prayer go through a range of emotions from delight to disinclination. Should we persevere, we find that if we take too little material to our prayers, we drift into dreamy silence. If we take too much, we become preoccupied with the words and fail to pray. The lifeboat might well come in the guise of what is called affective prayer. Only a soupçon of prayer material is required for this form of active contemplation. It is a case of "not too much, not too little, but just right," as a well-known advertisement of yesteryear used to proclaim.

We prepare for affective contemplative prayer by withdrawing to our secret place with a few set prayers, Scripture texts or whatever we deem to be necessary. We read them, consider them and feed on them one by one. As we mull over an item of prayer material, the soul is illumined by the love of God. We stay in the silence until the moment passes. Before long, the mind comes back down to earth and begins to wander. We move on to our next prayer or reading to help us refocus on God. When the mind is stilled, we immerse ourselves once more in the silence of love. And so we continue. In the periods of silence we are refreshed. When the mind wanders, we bring it to heel by returning to our prayer material. The more progress we make, the less material we need.

Something not unlike affective prayer is experienced in public worship, when songs are sung repeatedly. Those of a contemplative disposition find the repetition helpful. The songs still the mind while the soul is abandoned in worship. Those of a cerebral disposition, who want their minds to be fed by words and ideas, rather than being lifted up in praise, wonder why it is necessary to repeatedly sing the same words. But if the lover says to the beloved, "I love you," more than once, and the lovers are really in love, does the beloved look deep into the lover's eyes and say, "Don't be so boring!"?

The quiet Holy Communion service at 8 a.m. on Sunday morning is a magnet for contemplatives; so too is Cathedral evensong. When drawn to affective prayer, a few words or prayers will suffice whenever our minds begin to wander. When words fail to convey meaning and we are lifted up in silent adoration without any conscious effort on our part, pure contemplation has begun.

Consolations

The word "consolation" is used to denote an experience of the warmth, sweetness and joy in the climate of God's love.

St Teresa of Avila makes a distinction between two levels of consolation.

The first, *contentos*, is the experience of beginners. It is like a normal experience of human joy. It is a natural response to a favourable spiritual climate. It might be compared with the joy of the youngster who has been chosen for the football team, the student who has passed her exams with flying colours, or the moment we know that we have fallen in love. Beginners often experience such blessings in corporate worship, charismatic praise and when they withdraw into the secret place to find solitude and silence. Such consolations are easily disturbed by noise or interruptions.

The second type of consolation, *gustos*, is experienced by more advanced contemplatives. It is as if the sensors outside the house trigger the security lights in the middle of the night. We don't have to get up to turn them on. St Teresa of Avila considered such consolations to be spiritual rather than sensory. They may occur at any time. They aren't easily disturbed, and their durability is akin to St Teresa's concept of peace in daily tasks or the prayer of quiet.

It can't be said too often that it is unhelpful to go in search of spiritual feelings and blessings. What is of God will bless us anyway. What isn't will fade. If we don't set too much store by these sensations, we are unlikely to be deceived.

Consolations aren't evidence of holiness; they might even be God's encouragement to abandon our unholiness. Prayer isn't all sweetness and light. There are days when set prayer times seem to last forever. It is like being at work when there is little to do. Time stands still and even the big hand on the clock doesn't seem to move. If we make a patient effort to keep going, we unearth a paradox: there is no correlation between feeling mildly discouraged, apathetic or even desolate in a time set aside for prayer and the effectiveness of God's grace in the ensuing day. A muddled period of prayer, resolutely kept, is followed by a profitable day. As we look back on the day, we see that good fruit has emerged from what seemed to be chaotic prayer.

Junk mail

Even if we pray with unfailing regularity and do our best to live Godly lives, we won't be spared from obnoxious thoughts. This isn't because we are getting worse but because, as the mind is dredged, all kinds of refuse pops up from the bottom of the pond, which has previously escaped our attention and which we never dreamed lay buried beneath the deceptively still waters on the surface.

What is revealed is a by-product of plumbing the depths of the human soul. Our dismay at what comes to light is disconcerting. Sinful thoughts, rebellious ideas, anxieties and familiar temptations are vying to try to put us off our commitment to prayer. Don't be alarmed! Such assaults are the perfect antidote to pride. The remedy is to sit tight and humbly pray, "Lord have mercy on me a sinner."[7]

As we patiently set about the task of dealing with the debris we are not alone, for God in his love and mercy is entrusting us with a glimpse into the sink of the soul and the Holy Spirit will always be there to help us to clear up. Sometimes unwelcome thoughts and temptations can be firmly put aside and ignored. At other times, we register our disapproval by treating them as junk mail to be deleted. If all else fails, we become like a reed in the wind, duck down as low as we can and only get up when the coast is clear.

Confusion and focus

Just as the feisty schoolboy is confused when he finds that the rule, "i before e, except after c," doesn't always work, so those who enter the contemplative way are deprived of former certainties. When this happens, it is important to remember that God hasn't given up on us. In his love and wisdom he is leading us into deeper truth. As we advance in prayer, periods of uncertainty will issue in ever deeper faith and trust.

St John of the Cross issued a gentle warning about staying on course. We shouldn't stop to pick the flowers. It's easy to let the mind wander, but if we are to make any progress, we have to face up to the fact that prayer isn't always easy, and accept that difficulties are God's opportunities to help us grow in love and obedience. If we try to escape from spiritual confusion or aridity by going on mental jaunts, we will never clear the first fence.

Privation

St Francis de Sales[8] lay awake all night, feeling anxious. On reflection, he realised that this was the condition of the human heart when deprived of the assurance of God's presence. He saw that God sometimes allows us to feel abandoned so that we don't take his love for granted. He was surprised at how anxious he had become about a small matter and contrasted it with the times he had faced dangers, including threats to his life, while recalling that at such times he had felt secure in the peace of God.

Amongst those who set out on the journey of prayer, there is a good deal of confusion about the dark night of the soul, which can be clarified by turning to the teachings of St John of the Cross. In his writings, the primary aspect of the dark night[9] is being stripped. We are stripped of attachments to delight in all worldly things. This concerns all the natural senses of man. We are taught to walk by faith and not by sight and we have to come to terms with the fact that in this mortal life we see through a glass darkly. Being stripped of attachments is like struggling with someone who is pulling back the bed clothes on a cold winter's morning and urging us to get out of bed.

We also experience privation because, humanly speaking, God is unknowable. We come face to face with the great mystery that

God can't be fenced in by human language, thinking or imagining. The dark night is a continuing reminder that in this life we see through a glass darkly.

When St Francis de Sales saw that Jane Chantal[10] would find it painful to be without him, he anticipated her sense of pain and loss and prepared her for her suffering by writing a letter saying,

> "It is the object of the Transfiguration, my very dear mother, no longer to see Moses and Elijah, but Christ alone. To be able to be alone with one's King, to say to him, 'My beloved is mine and I am His.'"

Her reply to him, full of deep feeling and emotion, speaks of privation:

> "I see myself naked and deprived of all that was most precious to me. My God, my Father, how far the razor has penetrated! Blessed be he who stripped me. O God, how easy it is to leave what is around us, but to leave one's own skin, one's own flesh, one's own bones, and to enter into the intimacy of the marrow which is, it seems to me, what we have done, is a great and difficult thing, impossible except with the grace of God."

The three ways

Prayer is often divided into *the three ways*[11]: the way of beginners (which has been considered in Chapter Six), the illuminative way and union. These three ways can't easily be construed as a simple ascent because at times, the journey is more like the children's game of Snakes and Ladders.

The description of the beginner's prayer as the purgative way, a period of putting our house in order, can also be misleading because it seems to suggest that we can deal with sin once for all, whereas in reality the garden of the soul will never be completely free from weeds. Beginners establish a sound base of set prayer and try to amend their lives. They establish a simple rule and employ vocal prayer, arrow prayers, mantras, meditation and spiritual reading. From time to time there might be contemplative moments.

The illuminative way

The second of the three ways is called illuminative because it is held that the soul is enlightened. The transition to the illuminative way, about which I shall say more in the next chapter, is a key moment in the life of prayer and although it might pass by without much difficulty, for some it is a dramatic and painful experience. The illuminative way can be a long haul. Many will remain there for the rest of their lives.

As we enter the illuminative way, our eyes are spiritually darkened and we can't see. We feel that we can't pray because we can't meditate and our customary practices of prayer are found wanting. After the joys of the nursery slopes, the darkness is distressing. Having enjoyed beginners' blessings, we come face to face with bleak aridity. This aridity is not caused by indiscipline in prayer, sloppy living or serious sin. It is an important tool in the school of the Lord's service.

The darkening of our spiritual sight as we enter the illuminative way engenders fears that we can no longer pray at all. This blinding is a temporary condition caused by the intensity of the light of God's love. It's like the way our eyes respond when dazzled by the brilliance of the sun. When our eyes settle down we are enlightened. We begin to see more about the nature of God's love and deeper into truths about ourselves. This leads to a complete reappraisal of former attitudes and prejudices. We see that we are not nearly as advanced in the Christian life as we had hoped.

In the illuminative way our prayer changes. We gradually come to terms with being deprived of sensory joys and consolations and we experience a deeper peace and quiet. Secure in the love and mercy of God, we develop fresh insights into what is going on in the depths of the soul.

The dark night of the spirit

The next hurdle in prayer is the dark night of the spirit. Here we encounter an intense period of deprivation and a deeper yearning for God. In addition to the loss of sensory consolations and beginners' blessings, we are stripped of spiritual consolations. In the dark night of the spirit it is not uncommon to suffer spiritual impotence, unmerited hostility and feelings of disappointment with ourselves.

Union

Union is experienced by the few. It is described as a union in love and purpose. It is a process. If we say that a precious substance buried deep underground is at the heart of the earth, we have to acknowledge that it could be deeper, for to be at the very centre of the earth, it would have to be drawn to earth's molten core and annihilated. St John of the Cross saw that union becomes deeper as the soul is drawn deeper into God's love.

It could be argued that the words "unitive way" should be applied to the whole journey of prayer from the moment of our conversion and baptism. But so long as there is continuing resistance to God's love, so long as we allow our fallen human nature to call the shots, we are still in the two preliminary stages, the ways of beginners and proficients.

To be perfect is to have travelled as far as we can. Nevertheless, no one should rest on their laurels because there is always more to be done. It is said that when the life of prayer seems to be built on solid rock, God will test it by shaking it to the foundations.

A heart centred on God

As we advance on the spiritual journey, there are times when it might be likened to a James Bond car chase. We think that we have escaped from difficulties and trials but, as the cars race down the mountain side, we see that the baddies have taken a short cut and are trying to block the road ahead. At this point we struggle to cope. Although at an earlier stage we were only too happy to love and serve God, we now begin to think that we are no good. The truth eventually dawns. Our stubborn wills are still making conditions: I have married a wife, I have bought a field, I have a family or a good job – the excuses go on and on.

Eventually, we will see that without God we are empty vessels and so we fall down on our knees with the anguished cry, "Lord, without you I can do nothing."[12]

As we progress in contemplative prayer, we find that there is a continuing dialogue between the active and the passive. Sometimes we are actively praying; at other times we simply find ourselves at prayer. This thesis and antithesis produce a synthesis which is a continuing state of prayer filtering into every corner of our lives. Seeds of unceasing prayer are sown and take root. I have been particularly aware of such an under-lying state of prayer while conducting services, pastoral inter-views, in conversation, performing menial tasks and even while mowing the lawn.

Sometimes prayer is effortless. At other times it is costly. When it isn't easy to hold on, we are encouraged as we glimpse signs of the indelible prints of God's love on the soul. Prayer embodies and expresses our deep desire to love and serve God in his time and in his way. Many don't see it this way. The great Victorian apologist Cardinal John Henry Newman[13] wrote,

"The aim of most men esteemed to be conscientious and religious, or who are what is called honourable and upright men, is, to all appearance, not how to please God, but how to please themselves without displeasing him."

When we are drawn into contemplative prayer and leave the nursery slopes behind, first love is replaced by trials, incomprehension and a new round of temptations. The newborn within us robs us of our sleep, tries our patience and leaves us confused, because we don't always know what it wants.

Prayer doesn't come to an end when we struggle. This is where it begins.

Notes

1. Roy McKay. *John Leonard Wilson, Confessor for the Faith*. Hodder and Stoughton. London. 1973. p. 30ff. After the war one of Bishop Leonard's torturers, a militia man, became a Christian and Bishop Leonard was able to take him Holy Communion in the prison where he still had ten years to serve for war crimes.
2. From the hymn "And now O Father, mindful of the love." English Hymnal. No. 302.
3. 1 John 4.8 God is love.
   1 John 4.19 We love him because he first loved us.
   1 John 3.11 Love one another.
4. See "Heart of Compassion: Daily readings with Isaac the Syrian". Edited by A. M. Allchin. Darton Longman and Todd. 1989. p. 20. Isaac lived in Nineveh in the seventh century.
5. E. L. Mascall. *Grace and Glory*. SPCK. 1961. p. 46–47.
6. Luke 24.13ff.
7. Luke 18.13.
8. See Chapter Five note 6.
9. The dark night is not a life of misery but the astringent cleansing of the soul by the love and mercy of God. It is like having our knees scrubbed when we have fallen and cut them in the gravel.
10. Jane Chantal 1572–1641. Married Baron Chantal in 1592. On his death in 1601, she took a vow of chastity and from 1604 devoted her life to prayer under the direction of Francis de Sales.

11. The three ways. Those who persevere may pass on to the illuminative way, where contemplation becomes the normal mode of prayer. Those called to contemplative prayer are often called proficients or progressives. A few souls move on to union.
12. John 15.5.
13. John Henry Newman converted to Roman Catholicism in 1845, and spent the rest of his life in the Oratory in Birmingham.

Chapter Eight

Ride the storm

A Balaam moment

If we harden our hearts and refuse to listen to God, we will hear little more than our own inner voice which fuels self-love, chatters on about our own concerns, seconds our own proposals and stokes up self-regard or self-pity. If we have an inkling of what God wants us to do, but we sweep it aside and pay no further attention to what is required of us, sooner or later we will lose our way. Our spiritual progress will stutter and come to a halt, until we turn back to God and seek his help and assistance in getting back on track.

There is, however, another reason why we might feel that we have lost our way. This is what I call a Balaam moment. Balaam, you may remember from the tale in the book of Numbers,[1] was riding his donkey through a narrow gorge when it suddenly pulled up sharply and nearly threw him off. Furious, he dismounted and gave it a sound beating but it wouldn't budge, because an angel of the Lord was standing in the way.

Even if we are doing our best to serve God and have examined ourselves to see whether our difficulties are caused by our own wilfulness or unbelief, even if we have repented of our misusings of God's grace and are continuing to try to live the Gospel life, our prayer might still come to an abrupt standstill, causing us to feel as frustrated as Balaam.

Should we have done what we can to ensure that prayer hasn't failed because of our own negligence, we might find ourselves like the motorist who has done a quick check of tyre pressures, petrol, oil and windscreen washers before preparing to set out on a long journey. He sits in the driver's seat with his belt fastened and the engine ticking over, when he suddenly sees that the way ahead is blocked.

Is this a Balaam moment? Could it be a time for a complete change of direction?

If we are still trying to live Christian lives and are faithful in our commitment to prayer, we might find that we are stuck because we have encountered the point of transition to contemplative prayer, known as the ligature of the senses.

The ligature

Dom Chapman, the former abbot of Downside, observed that

> "most of the mystics (i.e. contemplatives) had always had the ligature of the senses since they began to meditate. One or two have vague recollections of meditative days. Hardly one of them knew he had the ligature till I told him."[2]

When I was a theological student, I hit what marathon runners call the wall. This is the moment when the runner breaks down after twenty miles or so and can go no further. I found that I couldn't meditate or pray. In times set aside for meditation I suffered a mental block. I tried vocal prayer. I tried discursive meditation. I tried spiritual reading. I made my confession. I tried anything and everything. Daydreaming didn't help. Pious thoughts were unfruitful and the words of spiritual books were as uplifting as a lead balloon. The spiritually juicy moments of beginners' consolations, the sensory joy in spiritual things, were a distant memory. In times of set prayer the written word caused a dull, confused block in my mind, which is hard to describe.

It didn't appear to be mental exhaustion or depression so I went to see my spiritual director, who spoke about the condition known as the ligature of the senses. He advised me to stop trying to meditate in set times of prayer and introduced me to the role of affective prayer, suggesting that I took the first tentative steps along the contemplative path.

I had reached a crossroads. It was as if God put up a hand saying "Stop!" and then signalled that it was time to travel in a different direction.

At the ligature of the senses, prayer comes to a sudden halt. It's not unlike the moment when the learner driver is thrown forward in his seat with a jolt, when the instructor jams on the brakes because he has noticed something the pupil has missed. Such a jolt is especially noticeable if we practise discursive meditation. The block is our inability to continue to use the intellect or imagination in prayer. Sensory responses to spiritual stimuli are numbed as if under a local anaesthetic. Nevertheless, although the soul is confined to a spiritual straitjacket, the will continues to be free.

What feels like failure in prayer is the work of God, urging us to leave the way of beginners and to move into the illuminative way. God is encouraging us to hold ourselves in his loving presence by a simple act of the will. If we persevere, we eventually find ourselves borne across the choppy waters of faith into the sea of contemplation.

This intuitive prayer isn't idleness. It isn't purely passive. Our intention to love and serve God is as strong as ever.

On approach

When we approach the threshold of contemplation, we are frustrated because we feel that we have lost the art of prayer.

Something is going wrong. It's like driving a car just before you run out of petrol, or the feeble sound on the radio just before the batteries go flat. It isn't easy to describe the emptiness or distaste for prayer we feel at this point of transition.

When we withdraw to the oratory of the heart and examine ourselves, we are pretty confident that our new-found difficulties have little or nothing to do with not trying hard enough, and we have already taken care to acknowledge and confess our sins.

Feeling helpless, we struggle on as best we can until we finally realise that we are being called to make a move. Like the Billy Goats Gruff in the children's tale, we are being invited to 'trip-trap over the wooden bridge' to feed in the lush green pastures on the other side of the stream. We hesitate because the ugly troll, who lurks beneath the bridge, is trying to put us off.

We might hesitate because we aren't sure if we have seen the signal to change direction and in any case we don't want to be parted from known and familiar ways of praying. To help us to decide how to proceed there are four questions we need to answer:

1. Do we still want to pray and do we really want God?
2. Can we still use mental and vocal prayer in our intimate converse with God?
3. Does the use of the intellect or the imagination help us to meditate and draw closer to God?
4. Are we in serious sin?

If the answer is "Yes" to the first question and "No" to questions 2, 3 and 4, it could be time to move.

The answers to these four questions help us to decide what to do. Even as we pray for help, a patch is put over the sensory eye so that the sight of the spiritual eye might be strengthened. There is nothing wrong with the sensory. It is good and of God. What defiles the man is not the sensory part of our human nature but something parasitic which lurks deep within the human psyche.

As we trundle along, we are so busy doing what we normally do, that we might well fail to notice the signal to change direction. In any case, our heads are drooping because nothing seems to have been of any help. Even the advice to take a book to our prayers is of little use because words become a blur. We feel like a tired student who appears to read while his mind is blank.

Nevertheless, at the ligature of the senses the soul isn't asleep. It's wide awake and not a little distressed. It's the senses which are dulled.

If we try to resist the ligature, it gets worse. We no longer find any profit in considering what the pearl of great price signifies, because this will block an intuitive insight into a truth which can't be put into words or contained in images. Public worship and private prayer might well leave us unmoved. Yet in the midst of our sorrow, we yearn for God.

Simplicity

Although our attempts to pray feel futile, we don't give in. We do the best that we can, while offering an aching heart to God.

As we sit at the bottom of the pit, brooding about our failures, we are taken by surprise as we begin to see that we have been led into this desert place by the Holy Spirit; that we are on an outward bound training course designed to help us to pray with greater simplicity.

In this wilderness, intimate moments with God are no longer enriched by the vividness of the imagination or the lucidity of the mind; rather, prayer morphs into an intense desire and longing for God, which cannot be fuelled by words or images.

The sufferings which accompany this moment of transition

provide us with an opportunity to grow in humility and trust. As we come to terms with what we thought were our failures, we discover that to be resolutely at our place of prayer, with a firm intent to pray, is the prayer. Just being there is the prayer. Just being there bears witness to our hunger for God. Even if the tiniest spark of desire for God remains tucked away in a hidden corner of the soul, we are still praying!

The seizing up at the ligature reminds me of the discomforts of a prayer walk from Lincoln to Digswell. After a couple of days, the muscles at the backs of our legs were so cramped that we could hardly move and we staggered around like drunken men. The angel of the Lord who came to our rescue was a physiotherapist, who coached us in stretching exercises. After her visit, whenever our muscles seized up, we painfully followed her instructions and slowly but surely loosened up before setting off down the road again.

At the ligature of the senses, we are like a caterpillar, twisting and turning as it wriggles and jiggles to ease its way out of its wrinkled and redundant skin, while adjusting to the dazzling light of new day.

On the threshold

It's hardly surprising that we don't like being deprived of the joys of the nursery slopes or that we are frightened of the unknown, but caution will stymie us if we dilly-dally on the threshold of the ligature of the senses. It's hardly surprising that we are none too keen to see our complacency, prejudices and former self-righteous attitudes exposed and challenged in the searching light of God's love, but it's important to press on.

A challenge

The challenges of the transition to the illuminative way are sensitively summed up in a little book by Olive Wyon[3]:

> "In prayer we have to go further. Meditation is a valuable aid to prayer, rather than prayer itself. Vocal prayer, though most important, is only one element in prayer. Sooner or later, people who have been practising these ways of prayer with great interest and profit, come to a standstill. The books they have been using now seem dull and meaningless. When they try to meditate it seems impossible. Yet, out of prayer times, their minds work perfectly well. They can think and write and attend to business with the same clearness and vigour as usual. But when they turn to prayer this power seems to have vanished completely. The time set aside for prayer becomes a period of vague discomfort, and they are glad when the time is up. Then they get worried. They think they must have committed some sin, or neglected some duty. They set to and wrack their brains to see where they have gone wrong.
>
> "This is a crucial moment in the life of prayer. For this is the beginning of the desert, in which they may have to wander for a long time. To go forward under such conditions demands a good deal of courage. At this point, for lack of wise guidance, many people go back: either they sink back to a rather formal level of religious duties, or they give up praying altogether."

At the crossroads

To help assess whether the ligature of the senses has been encountered, Dom Chapman applied the following test:

> "You know what it is like to say the Lord's Prayer slowly and devoutly with the result that you cannot imagine what it means. In the case of the 'Our Father', if it is not conscious distraction

that prevents your understanding the words, it is the ligature. The more devout you try to be," (*this is important, for the block of which he speaks may not occur unless we are devoutly at prayer*), "the more meaningless the words become. It may become impossible to even read a book or to pronounce the words of the office. It makes contemplatives into idiots for the moment, on occasions."[4]

Nevertheless, in the same way that a blind man is more sensitive to touch, taste and smell, so at the ligature our spiritual sensitivity becomes more acute.

Entering the illuminative way

In the transition into the illuminative way, being content to bear the pain of feeling unable to pray and offering our desolation to God, is a gold star prayer. Times when we struggle to pray are often highly productive. Led by the Holy Spirit and, where possible guided by wise counsel, we learn to abandon ourselves into the ocean of God's love, while relinquishing our attachment to former practices of prayer. We deal with unhelpful prejudices and unhealthy attitudes as they come to light. Prayer becomes simpler and more focussed. Formal meditation is replaced by loving attentive silence which might find expression in aspirations[5] and sighs, as we begin to emerge in the illuminative way. Meanwhile, the active dimension of contemplation is assisted by spiritual reading or the appropriate use of short prayers such as the Jesus prayer.[6]

In the same way that we suffer a loss of confidence at any period of transition in our lives, whether it is starting a new job, becoming a parent or retiring, so it is not uncommon to suffer a loss of nerve as we move into the illuminative way. Cast-iron certainties and unchallenged attitudes begin to outlive their usefulness. The inflexible Christian is no longer so certain that only his opinions or traditions are right and he humbly acknowledges that others who believe in the divinity of Christ find their own way home. The fundamentalist sees that his claims about literal Biblical certainties are not quite as certain as he supposed. The secularist, who bases his theology upon pure reason, discovers that he is after all a one-eyed Cyclops who can't understand the "Yes" of Mary, supposing it to be only a winter's tale. Buried away beneath the surface of our minds, we might be surprised to find a cocktail of all these prejudices.

St John of the Cross calls a certain wobbliness and uncertainty the *vertiginis spiritus*.[7] In the forecourts of the illuminative way we learn to walk again, for as we enter a new chapter in our spiritual lives, we learn to walk by faith and not by sight.

The flame of sacred love

In the contemplative life, we learn to care passionately about what is of concern to God and to sit light to some of our own presuppositions. As we grow in his love, our hearts are gradually set alight by the source of all love. As our souls are illumined by the Holy Spirit, we grow spiritually and are enabled to embrace new truths.

St John of the Cross suggests that the kindling of the fire of love in the hearth of the soul begins with the ignition of damp sticks, which represent our unyielding hearts and social conformities. They hiss and spit as they resist the flame of love. As the hissing and spitting begins to quieten down, the fire comes alive and the fuel begins to glow, giving off heat and light. When the fuel is ignited, it not only glows but comes to life in such a way that the flames begin a colourful dance and start to spread.

Contemplatives stoke the fire of love so that it burns ever hotter. Immersed in the love of God, they join the whole company of heaven in the continuing work of interceding for the world. They become part of an enterprise which makes many of our day-to-day concerns seem trivial.

A deep clean

Even if a man committed to prayer is the worst person in the community, he will almost certainly be better than he was before. But there is always room for improvement! It is not surprising, therefore, that in the illuminative way we embark upon a deeper level of self-examination.

We gradually come to terms with the fact that we have entertained a whole host of deadly sins in the parlour of the mind. Like Mr Scrooge, our eyes are opened. We see that we have been mean-spirited. We see that we are proud, self-righteous and hypocritical. We may not have overtly indulged in the sins of the flesh, but what about the underlying state of the heart? As for complacency, envy, fear and doubt – need I say more!

In the illuminative way, we see the shallowness of former trawls for sin. As we advance in the way of prayer, as we look more closely, we become more, rather than less, conscious of our sin. We feel worse, not because we are worse, but because our spiritual sight has improved. Our eyes are opened to the complexity and duplicity of our hidden motives. We had little idea that they played such an important role in stunting our spiritual growth.

In the clear waters of the ocean of God's love, we open our hearts to the God of love. It is only there that we find reassurance, as we discover that much of what we thought were sound principles were tired old prejudices. It is sobering to discover that if our unhealthy attitudes and prejudices are left to fester, they are corrosive. It is important to face up to them, rather than taking the broad way which opts for self-justification, blaming others or lightly brushing our imperfections aside.

Another ridge

As our eyes become accustomed to the light in the long trek through the illuminative way, we look up and mistakenly believe that we can see the summit of Mount Carmel, the mountain of prayer. We think we are nearly there! Our tired and weary limbs rejoice. But what appears to be the summit turns out to be simply the top of another ridge. There is still a long way to go!

But there are consolations. We find that our inability to meditate was not our own fault. We are reassured that moments of recollected silence weren't idle daydreaming but prayer. We find that as our minds are illumined by the Holy Spirit, we become more firmly established in the Christian faith. We no longer think of God as an interesting idea or the product of a myth, but know him to be very real. We begin to understand why Archbishop William Temple said he always struggled when invited to talk about proofs for the existence of God. We happily join those who taste and see that the Lord is good and we consider that trying to prove God's existence is as futile as trying to prove that you, dear reader, are still alive.

The terrible twins

Once we have settled down, we do well to remember that the two besetting sins of spiritual people are the terrible twins – pride and sloth.

Pride tempts us to take no notice of our failings and urges us not to look too closely into our hearts lest we are unsettled by weevils lurking within.

Sloth complacently yawns, while assuring us that it is far too much bother to tackle defective attitudes and prejudices. She suggests that we shouldn't be too hard on ourselves and makes a brilliant case for the defence, assuring us that we have every right to be angry, bitter or resentful. She persuades us that our failings are excusable and can all be laid at the door of others, before lightly spraying us with the charmed but deceptive scent of false humility to conceal any unpleasantness.

Sloth will spin any old yarn to conceal more serious sin, by delicately exaggerating a small fault. She might even hint that because God is almighty there is no real need to get up in the morning and go to work.

Sufficient grace

Our vocation is to pray in season and out of season. In spite of moments of desolation and difficulty, our desire and longing for God increases. As we persevere, we learn that it is in moments of testing and trial that we become fully aware of the grace of God.

If we lie awake at night wondering how we might cope with all kinds of hypothetical situations of our own imagining, we will soon be overcome with anxiety. The experience of the saints and the witness of our fellow Christians teaches us that "cometh the hour, cometh the help." Grace is there when it is needed, not before.

Loss

The dark night of the spirit is the next transition in the life of prayer. At this stage, our desire to pray is stronger than ever and we are not put off by periods of painful aridity. Just as we were deprived of the spiritual blessings of the senses (the beginners' blessings) in the transition to the illuminative way, so in the dark night of the spirit we are deprived of spiritual consolations. The emptiness is more acute than the pain of sensory deprivation but paradoxically it is a blessing, because it is the pain of yearning love.

Words of Jane Chantal[8] come to mind as I write these lines. She had suffered more than her fair share of trials, not least sufferings on account of her family and problems in establishing the Visitation. Distraught at the death of her mentor, Francis de Sales, she wrote,

> "My heart has never known so great a blow, but also it has never been so much at peace."

Painful emptiness encountered at critical moments in the way of prayer is like a bereavement. Someone very close has died and we touch the void. For a while, life itself seems to have lost all meaning. It isn't just the loss of companionship that troubles us, but the loss of a sense of purpose. For a while, everything seems drab and empty. We hardly notice the birds in the garden and are no longer thrilled by their song. It will be some time before the day comes when we look out of the window and see that the grass looks green again.

The aridity of the transition into the illuminative way is like the loss we feel when we are deprived of the warmth of human companionship. There is no one at home. There is no one in the kitchen or at the stove. There is no one in the garage, tinkering with the car. We are grief-stricken as we return to a bleak, empty house and see tokens of our former love – the photographs on the mantelpiece, the slippers by the hearth, a favourite jacket, the many little reminders of the one we have lost.

The aridity of the dark night of the spirit is more profound. We feel abandoned. We feel we have now lost God. The sense of absence leaves an aching void in the core of the soul. And yet, somewhere far beneath the pain, there is an enduring sense of peace. The absence is a presence. We turn to the Scriptures and read that even gold is tried in the fire.[9] As we weather the storm, we move into greater simplicity. It becomes easier to take the risks of faith because we are less reliant on the world's approval and we don't much miss it. Our determination to carry on is unabated.

Wisdom says, "Ride the storm and you will rediscover your beloved."[10]

Notes

1. Numbers 22.25ff.
2. Dom Chapman. *Spiritual letters*. Sheed and Ward. 1946. p. 114.
3. From Olive Wyon. *Prayer (An answer to How should I and How do I pray?)* Collins. Clear Type Press. 1962. p.115–117.
4. Dom Chapman. *Spiritual letters*. Sheed and Ward. 1946. pp. 61, 87, 114, 256 & 316.
5. An aspiration might be a sigh or a short exclamation. Aspirations simply escape! See Fr Augustine Baker. *Holy Wisdom*. Anthony Clarke Books. Wheathampstead. 1972. p. 456ff.
6. The Jesus prayer. In use from the fourteenth century. Now widely used by Orthodox Christians: "O Lord Jesus Christ, Son of God, have mercy on me a sinner."
7. *Vertiginis spiritus*. The soul feels confused and incapable of making moral judgements. This condition goes alongside the discovery that one's habitual way of prayer (for example discursive meditation) no longer helps but is a hindrance. The soul learns a proper distrust of its own judgement and relies in greater simplicity upon God.
8. Jane Chantal. See Chapter Seven note 13.
9. 1 Peter 1.6ff.
10. To ride the storm is to stop struggling – to go with the flow of God's will in prayer, to follow his lead rather than our own inclinations.

Chapter Nine

I knew I had a choice

When he was in the wilderness, being tempted by the devil, Jesus refused to turn stones into bread saying, "Man shall not live by bread alone but by every word that proceeds from the mouth of God."[1] For those who are distracted from pursuing the loving purposes of God by seeking for signs, wonders and miracles, he has cautionary words: "Do not rejoice in these things, but rejoice that your names are written in the book of life."[2]

Jesus at prayer

Jesus was the anointed Son of God. In a society which often fails to look beyond the purely secular, it is good to focus on how different our Lord is from ourselves, to reflect upon his divinity. And in a culture which overlooks the costly devotion of the saints, it is good to dust down the words of some of the traditional hymns – words such as

"We feebly struggle; they in glory shine."[3]

The extraordinary ministry of Christ was grounded in prayer. As we look in wonder at the drama of his preaching, healing, miracles, passion, death and resurrection, it's easy to overlook just how much importance he placed on ensuring that he was well prepared, that he had sufficient oil for his own lamp.

On fifteen occasions,[4] the Gospel writers tell us that Jesus was at prayer. Jesus spent long hours communing with the Father. Jesus was deep in prayer when the Holy Spirit descended upon him at his baptism. Jesus was illumined by prayer as he prepared for the appointment of his first disciples. Jesus escaped to places of solitude to seek the Father's will, so that he could be about his business. Jesus retired to a desert place or a mountain top, so that he might be spiritually strengthened and renewed for his costly ministry and mission.

The forty days Jesus spent in the wilderness open our eyes to the seriousness and intensity of the interior struggle in the conflict between good and evil. The radiance of his glory on the Mount of Transfiguration overwhelms us with such joy that our hearts sing out in songs and hymns of praise. The Gospels tell of his heroic struggle in prayer in the Garden of Gethsemane, as he tussled with the human will, and his agonising prayer on the Cross as he offered himself up as a perfect, once-for-all sacrifice. Finally, we reflect upon the account of the risen Christ praying for his disciples, blessing them and reassuring them, before his glorious ascension.

Union

The union of Father, Son and Holy Spirit is not simply a union of substance but a perfect union of love and purpose.

In the theology of prayer, however, the word "union" is a technical word which denotes the nearest anyone can come to God in this mortal life. It is the summit of the way of prayer. Union is a taste of heaven on earth, the fruit of an intimate relationship with God, grounded in love. This union has been likened to two candle flames being held together in such a way that they burn as one. Yet as the flames intermingle, the two candles remain distinct, for God and man continue to be two separate entities.[5] It is not a union of substance but a union of love and purpose. This level of spiritual intimacy is normally attained by those who have passed through the illuminative way and weathered the storms of the dark night of the spirit. It follows a long period in which the soul has endeavoured to die to the false self, while being prepared for a closer walk with God.

St Teresa of Avila wrote about a moment of awakening to the reality and importance of intimacy with God, when she realised that he is not just out there in the galaxies but deep within the human soul:

"In the beginning it happened that I was ignorant of one thing – I did not know that God was present in all things: and when he seemed to be so near, I thought it impossible. Not to believe that he was present was not in my power, for it seemed to me, as it were, evident that I felt there his very presence."[6]

If it is true, it is true, because it is true

God is present in the natural as well as in the spiritual. He is as present among the pots and pans as in the chapel. If God speaks to us in a dream or a vision, it is God speaking. If God speaks through the human mind, it is still God speaking. If God speaks to us through an intimation or an event, it is the same God speaking. If God speaks to us through mathematical truths or the scientific method, it is the same God speaking. If it is true, it is true because it is true.

St John of the Cross observed that the universal presence of God, including the presence of God in every human soul, is quite distinct from the conscious experience of the union and transformation of the soul in God by love.

Anyone can love God!

Those who are called to the summit of prayer are far from remote, speechless and ineffectual and are frequently to be found engaged in costly loving service.

St Catherine of Genoa was challenged by a monk,[7] who said she was a second-class Christian because her status as a laywoman was far inferior to his as a religious. The haughty fellow said that she would never acquire the merit he had acquired or be able to love God as profoundly as he did. Such a comment was addressed to a woman who had attained the higher reaches of prayer and abounded in good works. She is said to have lived in almost unbroken consciousness of the divine presence, and while continuing in this place of union, lived an extraordinary life of service to the destitute and sick and founded a hospital in Genoa.

St Catherine, like any truly saintly person, readily acknowledged that she was an unprofitable servant, but she left the monk in no doubt that he had overstepped the mark when he claimed that she would never be able to love God in the perfect way that he did. She wasn't amused. In fact, she was furious and shook her head so violently that all her hair fell down over her face as she expostulated that nothing, but nothing, could stop her from loving God.

A French mystic called Marie de l'Incarnation[8] wrote that in the state of union she was able to, "read, write, work and do what one will, and nevertheless this fundamental occupation always abides, and the soul never ceases to be united with God."

These two saintly women are reminders that we cannot readily separate being united with God in love from being united with God in purpose.

The picnic on the mountain

Shortly before I left the parish, I had a dream. A group of parishioners was seated on the green grass on the side of a mountain, enjoying a picnic. We had already climbed some way and had stopped for a break. After a while, I stood up to announce that I was going further on and invited those who felt called to join me to assemble. When I stood up, no one wanted to move. They signalled that I was to sit down and wait. So I did. For a while there was complete silence.

Some time later, I stood up again to say that I was about to go further up the mountain, and that I believed that there were some who were called to come with me. After a while, two or three stood up and together we began to move slowly up the slope in a light swirling mist.

My dream seems to have been about a call to a deeper level of prayer for all. Those invited to ascend were being called to leave their attachment to the things of this world behind so that, unencumbered, they might take the first steps up the slopes of contemplative prayer.

Shine as a light in the world

The way we spend our time is as important as the way we use our money. Both the Church and the world are richly blessed by those who respond to the call to turn even a portion of their precious time to contemplative prayer, to commune with God in order to be transformed by love.

Nevertheless, over many years, I have noted that even committed Christians don't always acknowledge the importance of prayer. Some see it as no more than a brief exercise, in which we spare a few moments to tell God what he already knows or to lamely ask him to support what we think is a good idea, before returning to what is supposedly the real world. This is feeble. If we want to move on in prayer, we must follow the example of Christ and love and serve God with energy and passion. As we identify the emptiness of our faith, hope and love, we beat upon the gates of heaven and beg God the Holy Spirit to come to our aid, so that rather than offering a limp handshake to the world, we radiate the warmth of God's love.

What contemplative prayer isn't

The goal of prayer is union with God in love and in purpose.[9] As I consider this great truth, I am mindful that I cannot find anything in the whole of the Gospel which suggests that the substance of prayer can be reduced to any outward practices, amazing inner states or unnatural physical postures. I cannot find anything about dazzling spiritual techniques or mystical trips. What I see is a constant emphasis upon the state of the heart.

Various disciplines and practices have their uses, and during the course of the life of prayer there are many blessings and consolations, but these are secondary. Outward practice is not worth a dime if it isn't undergirded by a heart centred on God. Authentic prayer isn't an outward show or a magic moment but an inner reality which produces good fruit.

When Jesus was asked by the disciples to teach them how to pray, he didn't advise them to

> gaze at candles
> light joss sticks
> take a tonsure
> lock themselves in a cell for twenty years
> go to Church every day
> wrap their legs around their necks

go around wearing a ball and chain
look starry-eyed and goofy
vacate their minds
hate their bodies
put their heads in their navels
starve
go on a pilgrimage
dress up in fancy robes.

He taught them the Lord's Prayer.

Only hearts ablaze with the love of God kindle flames of love in the hearth of the soul, so that self-righteous rectitude thaws like dripping icicles warmed by the spring sun, and hard-hearted hypocrisy is beaten flat on the anvil of God's love. Only hearts ablaze with the love of God will cause numerous little fires to ignite.

The account of the unshakeable faith of Bishop Polycarp,[10] who was martyred in the third century, is deeply moving. Roman soldiers came looking for the old man who was living in retirement. They had been ordered to burn him at the stake because of his allegiance to Christ. When they arrived, he hobbled out to greet them, and was courteous and friendly. He offered his executioners food and refreshment and humbly asked that he might be allowed to spend one hour in prayer.

The soldiers were clearly unhappy about their assignment and did their best to persuade him to deny Christ. All he had to do, they explained, was to burn a few grains of incense as a token of worship before a statue of Caesar, God of the Romans. "If you do this," they said, "it won't do any harm and your life will be spared." Polycarp's uncompromising refusal was accompanied by a robust profession of his faith in Christ:

"Eighty and six years have I served him, and he has done me no wrong."

God speaks to us today

My earliest conscious memory of the all-enveloping love of God was before I first went to school. I was lying in bed in Woodhouse Manor Farm in the Yorkshire dales, from where I could hear the waters of the River Dib, as it skipped and danced down a little valley into the River Wharfe. As I looked out of the bedroom window at a watery moon, I was conscious of the power of the love of God the Father within and all around me. I sensed that he was not just out there in the starry heavens but also with me and in me. Words fail as I try to describe this all-embracing presence. This is not, of course, the language I might have used at the time but the way I understand a precious moment, many years later.

It isn't easy to describe the extended communication which followed. At one level it was an intellectual vision. But in the same way that it is possible to move back and forth between vocal prayer and contemplation, so an intellectual vision which is communicated to the human spirit without words or images, might follow on from, accompany or precede a communication such as a dream or an imaginary vision.

What this extended communication seemed to be saying was that there would be two significant periods in my life. The first was clear: I was to play an active, caring and pastoral role in the years to come. I was in no doubt about the seriousness of this call which, somehow or other, I knew to be connected with the story about Joseph[11] and the provision of corn in Egypt. At one level I had no idea what this communication could mean and yet at another, I fully understood. Although I heard no words, I knew that I was being invited to give my assent.

The second, more significant part of the vision seemed to be hidden behind a veil of secrecy. I cannot begin to describe the sense of the mystical power of the silent love which filled me, enfolded me and surrounded me. Having attained my three score years and ten, I have no doubt about the reality of the presence of the living risen Christ and the promise of the life of the world to come.

There were no words or images but awesome silence. I was quite content to take this communication on trust. I also fully understood that it was neither possible nor desirable for me to comprehend, nor was it safe for me to know what lay so far in the future. I was being shown that there was to be a second calling. I am still not certain what it is, but it could be a vocation to contemplative prayer. However, of one thing I am quite certain: deep in my heart, I said yes to both callings.

Holy Week

As I reflect upon the scene outside the village church, where Ross the donkey stood wrapped in bandages and surrounded by people singing their hosannas to the Son of David, I give thanks to God for the many years in which I was surrounded by praising people filled with holy joy. I give thanks and praise to God that like Ross, we were there. But I am also deeply conscious that the lifetime journey of prayer takes us beyond the flag waving of Palm Sunday as, little by little, it leads us into the mature and costly discipleship of Holy Week, where we come to a deeper understanding of the victory of the Cross and the vocation to die to self. It is true that the disciples were to be seen in the Temple, continually praising God; but this was for a little while. It was not long before they were sent out to the uttermost parts of the earth to spread the good news of the Gospel.

Being stripped of the many good things on which we are overdependent is costly, but deprivation isn't negative. God in his love and wisdom doesn't strip and deprive us of the values of this world because they're no good, but because they aren't the best. In the life of prayer, we learn that we aren't just called to give up the bad for the good, but the good for the better, and the better for the best. In the privacy of the oratory of the heart, we learn painful but invaluable lessons: we learn to be content to be stripped of our clinging to the good, the bad and the indifferent, while preparing ourselves for the moment we are called to leave all our baggage behind, as we stand at the gates of heaven.

Paradoxically, in dying to self we find our lives. We cast our bread upon the waters and find it after many days. God, in his love and wisdom, will give back so much more than we have offered up. The willingness of Jesus Christ to be stripped of life itself did not end in death, but in new life. He was not destroyed on the Cross. This is where the victory was won and his glory seen.

One dark night

When I was about eight years old, I was unwell. I had pneumonia. I can still see the concern on my mother's face when she saw that my temperature had already reached 105°F. It must have been a cold winter's evening, because the room was illuminated by the glow of one of those old-fashioned electric fires which shed a dim light in my darkened bedroom.

In the dark hours of the night I went on a journey. For a while it seemed that I was speeding weightlessly down a long dark tunnel. I travelled for some time. The curious thing is that although it was pitch black, I could see. My mode of travel was not unlike a man floating about in a spacecraft. I was surprised that I didn't feel apprehensive, but still and calm in the peace of God. I knew that it was all right. I knew that all was well, and that "all manner of things would be well."[12]

When I came to a halt, I found myself beside a closed door or gate. It was the simple door of the sheepfold. In my spirit I knew that this was a place of transition. It was the gate of heaven. It was nothing like the pearly gates but simple, honest and unadorned.

I realised that I had stopped clinging to life and had crossed over to the other side. I wanted to stay. Many might find it difficult to understand my desire to stay, rather than to return. But the deep experience of love, joy and peace was something I never wanted to lose. After a period of sickness when I had been confined to bed feeling weak and ill, the world had become remote and distant. In such a condition I had suddenly found myself caught up and given a taste of bliss. I had no desire to cling to life, but wanted to let go and enjoy the riches of heaven.

I hadn't enjoyed the glories of peace for very long when I heard a clear locution. The words spoken were gentle, firm, loving and purposeful: "It's too soon. I want you to go back." God, in his love and wisdom, had other plans. It wasn't yet time to let go of life. I was in no doubt that it was the Father's will that I should return to the world.

After the locution there was silence for a while but as soon as the words were spoken, I knew I had a choice.

I felt myself gently carried back over the threshold of life and some time later, I awoke from a deep sleep, to see my mother and the doctor standing by my bed.

In my extra time, I have rejoiced that God is perfect love, that we are lovable and that he has prepared for those who love him such good things as pass man's understanding.

In his Gifford lectures in Glasgow before the war, William Temple said that

"the true aim of the soul is to glorify God; in pursuing that aim it will attain to salvation unawares."

He continued,

"Salvation is the state of him who has ceased to be interested in whether he is saved or not, provided that what takes the place of that supreme self-interest is not a lower form of self-interest, but the glory of God."[13]

123

The celebration of the glory of God is one of the great attractions of King David[14] who, in spite of all his failings, proclaimed:

> 'Glory and honour are in his presence,
> strength and gladness are in his place.
> Give unto the Lord, ye kindred of the people,
> give unto the Lord glory and strength.
> Give unto the Lord the glory due unto his name:
> bring an offering, and come before him:
> worship the Lord in the beauty of holiness.
> Blessed be the Lord God of Israel for ever and ever.'

> And all the people said, Amen,
> And praised the Lord.

Notes

1. Matthew 4.4.
2. Luke 10.20. See also Revelation 21.27.
3. From the hymn 'For all the saints'. English Hymnal No 641.
4. S. D. Gordon. *Quiet talks on Prayer*. Echo Library. 2007 p. 88ff.
5. St John of the Cross. The Ascent of Mount Carmel. Book ii chapter 5.
6. Teresa of Avila. Interior Castle M. Starr. Riverhead Books. Penguin Group inc New York. pp. 123–124.
7. E. L. Mascall. *Grace and glory*. SPCK. London. 1961. pp. 56–57.
8. Marie de l' Incarnation 1599–1672. Pioneer of education in the new world, who combined contemplative gifts with practical initiatives.
9. St John of the Cross. E. W. Trueman Dicken. *The Crucible of Love*. Darton, Longman, and Todd. London 1963. p. 355ff.
10. Polycarp circa 69–155AD. Bishop of Smyrna. He was arrested at a pagan festival soon after returning from Rome. The Martyrium Polycarpi gives an account of his trial and martyrdom.
11. Genesis 43ff.
12. Julian of Norwich. *Revelations of Divine Love*. Penguin classics. 1966. Chapter 32 p.109.
13. Canon A. E. Baker. *William Temple and his Message*. Penguin Books. 1946. p. 98.
14. 1 Chronicles 16.27–29 & 36.

Postscript

"No one doubts," wrote E.W. Trueman Dicken in 1963 in his preface to *The Crucible of Love*, "that faith in this country today is in a period of comparative recession. A very proper attitude of self-criticism prevails among Christians, however, and many and various remedies have been proposed and tried in an effort to regain the lost ground. Curiously the one remedy which our Lord has promised to crown with success, although not necessarily in any worldly sense, has yet to be seriously put to the test – prayer! The generality of English Christians frankly give very little time and energy to prayer, have little confidence in its power and are pitifully ignorant of what it entails."

"This book," he continued, "is written in the belief that whatever else we may do to recall our nation to God, prayer is the ultimately indispensable key to the situation. Further it is axiomatic that if we are to pray, we must know how to pray; and we cannot reasonably demand the help and guidance of the Holy Spirit in this, if we neglect the obvious aid he has already given us in the writing of the spiritual masters. By a continuous tradition all down the centuries, these teachers of prayer built up, tested, and handed on the accumulated experience of millions of prayerful and saintly Christians."

Appendix

Spiritual communications

God speaks to us in many ways. In the life of prayer it is important to acknowledge that he speaks to the whole man, body, mind and spirit. He speaks through revealed truth. He speaks to the heart. He speaks through the imagination. He speaks through events and he speaks in and through dreams, visions, locutions, intimations and intuitions.

Events

In our secular society we have lost sight of the way God speaks to us through events. These might be of global significance – like a banking crisis – or of more immediate relevance to our own lives. In prayer, we begin to see more clearly the way that our simple obedience to God, even in little matters, bears good fruit. It is important to keep our eyes open for the way that God speaks to us individually, as well as reading the signs of the times.

Locutions

Locutions are interior words which transcend our own human thinking. They might present as clear words – for example, I was at prayer considering where to find a house for a priest when I had a locution: "Go down to The Hardings." Within an hour I had found the necessary house. This was what is called a successive locution because it followed on from my particular prayers and petitions.

Formal locutions appear to have no connection with what we are doing. For example as I returned from holiday I received a locution: "Your ministry in Braughing is finished." I had no plans to leave, but within a month I had been approached about a move.

Substantial locutions are deeply embedded in the soul. St Paul's life was transformed when he heard a voice saying to him, "Saul, Saul why are you persecuting me?" (Acts 9.4).

Locutions might be heard like a real voice, occur as a thought in the mind or be as if a word was spoken.

Intimations and intuitions

Intimations and intuitions might be described as nods and winks. On occasions, we just know that something is true or that we have to do something today. By attending to small matters we learn whether such intimations or intuitions are genuine by their outcomes, but in more important matters careful discernment is required.

Visions

Visions can be divided into three categories:

> Corporeal
> Imaginative
> Intellectual

In a corporeal experience we see something as if it is really there. The angel isn't a vision in the mind but is standing there in front of us.

The imaginary vision presents images on the screen of the mind. It is an interior experience.

The intellectual vision is more purely spiritual, by which I mean that no words are spoken, no sound is heard, and yet there is a clear communication which can subsequently be understood by the mind and expressed in verbal form. One way to describe it is to say that it is like a mutual understanding which is so profound that it is communicated without words or images. A glance is all that is required. In an intellectual vision, the meaning of the glance is clearly understood and the impression might well endure for a long time.

Discernment

It is important to try to discern what comes from where. Communications can be complex and multi-layered so it isn't always easy. A dream, vision or locution might be God speaking to us through the natural human activity of the mind, but it might be the product of our own thoughts.

In other words, dreams, visions and locutions often speak to us but from time to time, they are of special spiritual significance. In order to see what comes from where, we may hold up what is received to the light of the Gospel of Christ and measure it with the wisdom of Christian teaching. Experience and prayer teach us that an authentic spiritual dream, vision or locution has a different feel about it. It bears the hallmarks of Christ and leaves a legacy of love, joy or peace. Of course, it is also found to be true.

In order to help us to find our way through the maze of communications, we pray for gifts of discernment and ever greater humility, while clearing the decks by doing our best to set aside our own agendas.

Dreams, visions, locutions and other spiritual communications engage the whole man, body, mind, and spirit. What is received can only be understood and communicated by the human mind and the human voice. Even an experience of emptiness can only be understood and communicated in this way.

Bibliography

A. Baker. *Holy Wisdom.* Anthony Clarke Books. Wheathampstead. 1972.

R.M. Benson. *Spiritual Letters.* A.R. Mowbray. London and Oxford. 1924.

J.P. De Caussade. *The Sacrament of the Present Moment.* Font paperbacks. 1966.

John Chapman. *Spiritual letters.* Sheed and Ward. London. 1946.

F.L. Cross. *Studies in the Fourth Gospel.* Christ Church. Oxford. 1957. Article by G.L. Phillips p 83.

F. De Sales. *On the Love of God.* Image books. New York. 1963.

F.P. Harton. *The Elements of the Spiritual Life.* SPCK. 1932.

Jones, Wainwright, and Yarnold. *The Study of Spirituality.* SPCK. London. 1986.

K. Kavanagh. *St John of the Cross. The Collected Works.* ICS publications. Washington DC. 1979.

E.L. Mascall. *Grace and Glory.* SPCK. 1961.

T. Merton. *Seeds of Contemplation.* Burns and Oates. 1949.

T. Merton. *Spiritual Direction and Meditation and What is Contemplation?* Anthony Clarke. Wheathampstead. 1975.

J.H. Newman. *The Grammar of Assent.* Image Books. Doubleday and Co USA. 1955.

P. Pourat. *La Spiritualité Chrétienne* vols i-iv. Paris Libraire Lecoffre. J Gabalda et fils Editeurs. 1931.

E.K. Sanders. *Francis de Sales 1567–1622.* SPCK. 1928.

E.K. Sanders. *Jane Chantal. 1572–1641.* SPCK. 1928.

Teresa of Avila. *The Way of Perfection.* Sheed and Ward. London. 1977.

Teresa of Avila. *The Interior Castle.* Riverhead Books. New York. 2003.

E.W. Trueman Dicken. *A Study of the Mysticism of St Teresa of Jesus and St John of the Cross.* Darton, Longman and Todd. London. 1963.

E. Underhill. *Mysticism.* Methuen and Co Ltd. London. 1911. Revised 1930.

O. Wyon. *Prayer.* Collins Fontana books. 1962.

Lightning Source UK Ltd.
Milton Keynes UK
173633UK00001B/148/P